Where the Twenties Weren't Roaring

Where the Twenties Weren't Roaring

Catherine Dycus

Brunswick

Cover art and text illustrations by Terry Cox-Joseph.

Library of Congress Cataloging-in-Publication Data

Dycus, Catherine, 1920-
    Where the twenties weren't roaring / Catherine Dycus.
    -- 1st ed.
        p.   c.m.
    ISBN 1-55618-198-1 (pbk. : alk. paper)
    1. Country life--Kentucky--Anecdotes. 2. Kentucky
--Social life and customs--20th century--Anecdotes.
3. Dycus, Catherine, 1920---Childhood and youth--
Anecdotes. 4. Kentucky--Biography--Anecdotes.
5. Kentucky--Rural conditions--20th century--Anecdotes.
6. Dycus, Catherine, 1920---family--Anecdotes.
7. Vacations--Kentucky--History--20th century--
Anecdotes. 8. Hammond (Ind.)--Biography. 9. Chicago
Region (Ill.)--Biography.   I. Title.

F456.D94 2001
976.9'042--dc21
                                        2001037632

First Edition
Published in the United States of America
by

Brunswick Publishing Corporation
1386 Lawrenceville Plank Road
Lawrenceville, Virginia 23868
434-848-3865
http://www.brunswickbooks.com

Dedicated to the memory of:
Mom and Dad,
Grandma Bell,
and Ivy Brasher

Acknowledgments

This book would not have grown without the help and advice of many, whom I would like to thank. First of all, Mrs. Doris Gwaltney, teacher, mentor, and friend who led the writing class in which this work was born, encouraged me to publish it, and advised me during the process.

Also my brother, James Dycus, and my cousin, Lucille Duncan Castleberry, who were invaluable aides in verifying or amending my statements, or adding details of which I was unaware or had omitted; then too, Brother Bill, who shared my experiences if not always my point of view.

Mr. Odell Walker, Lyon County Historian and former president of the Lyon County Historical Society, who encouraged me and persuaded the staff of the Lyon County newspaper, *The Herald Ledger*, to print the stories that were finished at that time. Also Ms. Anita Baker, Editor of the newspaper, *The Times Leader*, printed in Princeton, Kentucky, who published the hunting story under a different title.

My friend, Irvene Seney, who was the final reader and principal editor of the manuscript prior to publication.

Terry Cox-Joseph for the cover art and illustrations, and Brunswick Publishing Corporation for their guidance through the business.

Becky Fontaine, Kim McHugh, and Elaine Ball, the readers and critics who helped fine-tune the work, and Sarah

Wade Owen and Mercedes Crum who assisted during the early writing.

Brock Robertson and Ted Darby for help with major computer catastrophes, and friend, and neighbor, Sandy Cobb for help with the minor ones.

For finding examples to back up the illustrations Sarah Wade Owen, Goldia Parish, Mrs. Teddy Holt, Daisy Holt, Katrina Kennedy, Betty Polk, Georgette Beatty, Anita Harrell, Mary Stuart Mason, and Katherine Freakley.

Help in recalling names of residents of the community during the period of my writing came from Margaret Hooks, Edna Conger, and Mary Bob Riley.

Great thanks is due those who encouraged me along the way: my sisters-in-law, nieces and nephews, all my good friends and, particularly, members of the writer's class.

Immeasurable gratitude to everyone!

Table of Contents

Preface

When I signed up for the class "Writers: Family Historians at Work," sponsored by the Lifelong Learning Society of Christopher Newport University, and taught by Mrs. Doris Gwaltney, I did not expect this book to be the outcome. I had expected to find some forebears whose lives and times I could recount for my own satisfaction and the edification of my nieces and nephews, current, grand, and great.

Unfortunately, my ancestor hunting was not too successful. The family tree was really a bush, but the writing class was going on.

For some of us "Family Historians" who were floundering for something to write, Mrs. Gwaltney gave us projects that we might use to get started. One day she suggested that we write about an interesting vacation. Then I remembered that getting to our "Vacation" was an interesting experience in itself. I started writing and one memory led to another.

The family vacations I have written about are those centered on visits with relatives in western Kentucky during the summers of 1926, 1927, 1928, and 1929.

To create a sense of unity I grouped the stories into what I feel is a natural sequence. All the experiences that I have related are true and as accurate as my memory has pictured them. However, since some of the activities took place every year, I used several different occurrences relating to one activity in the same story to sustain interest. To keep the characters real, I have made their actions and conversations resemble what they would have done or said at that time.

For accuracy I have called on my older brother, James, and my cousin Lucille Castleberry to confirm or correct my statements. On occasion they have added extra details for what I had written.

Writing these memories has brought a lot of pleasure to me. I hope that those who read them will be reminded of their past. The narratives may draw a picture of life in another era for those who know only the present or can remember only the recent past. I recall with love all those who were named, and many who were not named, whose presence helped create the basis of these stories.

CHAPTER I

The Roaring Twenties

The Charleston and the Black Bottom, frenetically danced to jazz music by ladies with bobbed hair and short skirts, bootleg liquor and bathtub gin, wild parties and loose women were earmarks of the era called the "Roaring Twenties." In those days people blatantly ignored or found ways to circumvent the laws prohibiting the use of alcoholic beverages. The wealthy and the "New Rich" invested their money and squandered their dividends. Headlines in our hometown paper and *The Chicago Tribune* chronicled the exploits of the times.

Even though we lived in Hammond, Indiana, an industrial suburb of Chicago, it would have been hard to convince Jim, Bill, and me that we were growing up amidst all that hubbub. We didn't read the newspapers. We were busily exploring our yard and the vacant lots surrounding our house, watching the construction of new houses being built nearby, and playing with the children that moved into them.

The way of life depicted in the news distressed Mom and Dad. In the evenings when all the family was in the house during supper and before bedtime, we children heard them make disparaging remarks about the flappers, speakeasies, gambling, raids, and arrests featured in the papers.

They had grown up in Lyon County, a rural area in western Kentucky where the precepts of their local churches and the principles expressed in the McGuffy's Readers they studied as children molded their concepts of moral and civil behavior. As adult schoolteachers they lived by the same precepts and taught the same principles from the same books. Their lives in Hammond centered on our home, Dad's work, the church, the P. T. A., and local politics.

By the time I was born, Dad had left teaching for a position in the office of a small chemical company. He had a year-round job and two weeks vacation. Even though they had moved to Hammond for better financial opportunities, they deeply regretted leaving the relatives and friends that remained in Kentucky.

The booming economy that affected the cities did not extend to rural America. Each year Mother and Dad looked forward to Dad's vacation so they could go "back home" where they could be again among those they loved and experience again the calmer, saner life from which they had come, a place where the Twenties weren't roaring.

CHAPTER II

Going "Back Home"

Late each spring an air of excited anticipation walked into the house when Dad came home from work and gave Mom the dates of his vacation — most often it would be in August. Mother sent a flurry of letters to relatives and friends in Kentucky. She and Dad eagerly awaited the plans and the news in the replies. Their news didn't impress me much because I was still in kindergarten at school and busy playing at home and really didn't think about "August."

However, once mother began to put aside my ironed Sunday dress, Jim's best knickers and Billy's little suit, I too became excited. It meant that soon we would go to see Uncle Billy and Aunt Nancy and Aunt Linnie and Uncle Herman in Kentucky where every day seemed to bring a new adventure.

Mother was particularly concerned about clothes. There was so little space for them. Our things had to be packed in two suitcases, one for us children and Grandmother and one for Mom and Dad. Fortunately, we needed only one set of "Sunday" clothes each. A couple of work shirts and a pair of work pants added enough for Dad. A few housedresses and walking shoes completed the needs for Grandmother and Mother. A couple of pairs of overalls, some everyday shirts, and tennis shoes each were generally sufficient for the three of us children. I also had to have either a skirt and blouse or a second-best dress to wear when we went "visiting."

Eating places were scarce along the road, so we had to take our food and eat picnic style. Mother fried chicken and made ground beef, and ham salad to wrap and pack in a box with eggs and bacon and bread. She would place it beside her feet on the floor at the front where it would stay as cool as possible. Billy was too short for his feet to touch the box. (Six-packs and ice coolers were unknown to us at that time.) Cooking and eating utensils were put in another box. A couple of extra quilts or blankets had to be stowed somewhere in the car. The wind blew on everyone in the back seat. If the weather turned cool, Grandmother, Jim, and I would need cover.

Dad had to see that the car was in top shape. He cleaned spark plugs, checked all the wires, and changed oil. He also inspected brakes and tires, especially the spare.

We had a black Chevrolet with a body shaped much like a buggy. Fenders were rounded over the wheels and attached to the running boards that ran along each side. The doors came up to my shoulder at both the front and back seats. A heavy cover supported by a metal frame ran from the back of the rear seat up over the top of the car and fastened at the front over the windshield. It was very stiff with a coating of some thick black substance that gave it body and helped it resist minor damage from branches, rocks and strong wind. It had a panel of glass that one could see through in the back over the rear seat. The windshield itself was made of two panels of glass. Although the top panel could be opened, I never saw Dad open it.

The motor was out in front covered by a hood. Each side of the hood had ventilating slits and was hinged so it could be raised and folded back from over the motor if there was engine trouble (and somewhere there would be). The radiator was kept sealed with a metal cap on top. Headlights were fastened to the front fenders.

The wheels were about 30" in diameter and had big wooden spokes. Tires were about three or three and one half inches in diameter with a rubber innertube inside.

We were to take Route 41, a new numbered highway under construction. It began somewhere in the north of Wisconsin, came through Chicago, went through Hammond, Indiana, our hometown, and proceeded through almost every small town in western Indiana. It crossed the Ohio River, went through Kentucky and on down to Florida. Dad knew we would be jarred by every bump and swayed at each right- or left-angled turn from Hammond to Henderson, Kentucky, where we would leave it for U.S. 60, another highway going toward Paducah.

The surfaces of Route 41 were not yet uniformly laid. Most of the road was of gravel. Cement pavement began near and went through the towns and cities. Posted speed limits were from five to twenty-five miles an hour in town and thirty-five to forty-five miles an hour on the open road.

Several of the cities through which we would pass had brick pavement, fairly dustless when it was dry, and good and firm when it was wet, but very uneven and bumpy in any weather. Over the years the town I learned to recognize, even when I was half-asleep, was Vincennes. Dad said it had cobblestones for pavement. From the way it felt I think they were the same ones that lined the streets when George

Rogers Clark and his backwoodsmen captured the town during the Revolutionary War. The car rumbled, jiggled, shook, and rattled there as it did in no other town.

When we finally left, I have dim impressions of being awakened during the night and being tumbled into my clothes, groggy and still half-asleep, while being urged to hurry up, "It's almost four o'clock. Dad wants to get on the road." To me, in the process of being rousted out of a deep sleep, the trip was an ordeal to go through to get to the "Vacation."

Mother had packed the suitcases before bedtime. They, the cooking utensils and some other things were all placed on the running board, covered with oil-cloth, and tied with clothesline rope to the rear door of the car and the expandable package carrier which was attached to the running board and left-hand rear fender. Mother and Dad had been up since about three o'clock stowing them. Some items had also been fastened to the spare tire on the back of the car.

How we all crowded into the car is not clear to me. I think that Bill, being the smallest, was up front with Mom and Dad. Grandma Bell, Mother's mother, sat on the left in the back seat. I, only vaguely aware, clambered up into the middle beside her. Jim was settled on the right.

Grandma must have let me sleep with my head in her lap because I can only remember rumbling and jiggling along in a semi-conscious state. At one point I opened a bleary eye to see an orangish glow in the sky to the east of a long grassy stretch of pasture and dropped off to sleep again. I was restless because each road surface provided a different type of rumble or rattle and I was roused until, becoming inured to the new noises, I slept again.

When the sun had risen high enough to dry the dew off the grasses beside the highway, Dad found a little wooded spot where we could stop for breakfast. Only a few scrub oaks and hazelnut bushes provided shade, but there were plenty of weeds for tinder and enough sticks from fallen branches to make a small fire. Mother, Grandmother, and I went off to one side where the bushes were thickest to take care of our physical needs. Dad and the boys went off in another direction and came back with the sticks for the fire.

While Mother got out the cooking equipment, Grandmother spread a picnic cloth on the ground and got out the basket of old plates and steel knives and forks. Dad scraped a spot clean of leaves or grass and scooped out a little saucer shaped depression in the middle of it. He built a fire there and placed a little larger piece of wood on each side of it, just far enough apart to hold the blue granite enameled coffeepot and the old iron skillet. We had bacon and eggs, fresh ones carefully packed so they wouldn't break, bread toasted in the skillet, and coffee. (We children had milk from a thermos bottle. It was cool, sort of, not really cold, but we knew not to complain.)

When we finished, everything was wiped thoroughly and re-packed. Mother would wash the eating utensils wherever we stayed that night.

Dad carefully poured the leftover coffee and some water over the fire. "I fought enough brush and forest fires when I was growing up on the farm to last a lifetime. We surely don't want to start one here."

He began kicking dirt over the smoldering ashes. Bill and I tried to help; however, we only succeeded in kicking up a lot of dust. Jim and Dad managed to scrape up a good pile of dirt over the embers before Dad emptied the rest of the jug of water on it all.

A few miles up the road Dad saw a grocery store with a pair of wooden outhouses at the back and two gas tanks in the front. We spied the outhouses, a big improvement over the bushes we had used.

We were near Kentland, almost eighty miles from home and the car needed gas. Dad stopped by the gas tank, a tall red metal column with a long lever on one side and a hose on the other. Above that was a clear glass tank with markers at regular intervals, like a ruler. It was supported by a few red upright bars attached to a rounded cap. Atop it all was a beautiful crown of white glass decorated in red. It was called a "Red Crown," the company logo for the Standard Oil Company. I can remember the man's hand going back and forth with the long pump handle as the gasoline rose past the red marks while the liquid filled the clear glass container near the top. Then I watched the liquid fall as it passed the red marks measuring each gallon being drained into the tank of the car. I thought the tanks were beautiful and was always happy when Dad bought this kind of gas.

Dad also checked the oil (he usually had to add a quart,) and the tires, (they usually needed a little air in one and some released from another). The man also filled our water jug and handed it to Dad as we piled back into our places and drove off.

When we children got restless, Mother would start up some silly song like "It Ain't Gon'na Rain No More" or "Ruben Rachel" and we would all join in. Soon Jim would begin one of the scout camp songs like "John Jacob Jingleheimer Schmidt." And so it would go. In later years we would sing the songs in parts. Mother would carry the tune and the rest would harmonize, Dad and Jim on bass and tenor, Bill and I on the alto, and occasionally one of us on a tenor obbligato. I particularly enjoyed these times. In my opinion we sounded pretty good too!

Sometimes we would read Burma Shave signs. Each of us would try to be the first to spot the next one. "COLLEGE BOYS" "YOUR COURAGE MUSTER" "SHAVE OFF" "THAT FUZZY" "COOKIE DUSTER" "BURMA

SHAVE." When that interest faded, Mother or Dad would tell us stories or point out interesting things along the road. We would count silos, note unusual markers in cemeteries, notice farm animals, and check the various crops, particularly the tall corn.

Somewhere near Attica we stopped again for lunch — sandwiches this time, ground beef or ham salad. We would have stopped for gas somewhere and picked up some soda pop to go with the sandwiches. We were allowed a fruit flavored drink. Billy usually got grape or strawberry. I almost always got cherry. Jim would usually get Nehi Orange. We weren't allowed to drink Coca-Cola. It was considered almost as wicked to drink as beer or whisky. (At that time, I believe, there was actually some derivative of cocaine in the coke formula.)

After Attica there was a long stretch of low-lying road that ran across, between, and beside first one and then another of the many creeks and rivulets that wound their way into the Wabash River. At that point it ran due south near the western edge of the state off a few miles to our right. At Veedersburg, the road began to twist and curve, on an almost level path until it came close to Rockville. From that point on, for several miles, we sat with nerves on edge.

There were hills in western Kentucky. There was a so-called mountain by the Kuttawa Mineral Springs. Mother and Dad had ridden over both the hills and the mountain on horseback, in a wagon, and in a buggy. However, they were not prepared for this.

At first the road began to climb a little and began to curve and twist. It was almost like our own private roller coaster, great fun until the route got steeper and steeper and the ground beside the highway dropped precipitously farther and farther down. The car would struggle up and around a curve on the right and swerve around a curve and halfway up a hill to the left then zoom down a slope before struggling up and over the next rise. Gradually the motor began to steam and cough. Dad worried about the engine getting hot. Suddenly as we were chugging up a long steep hill we spotted a restaurant.

It was a big tall building, rounded on the front with huge windmill sails toward the top. A high wooden fence that ran along the hillside next to it bore large painted letters "JUNGLE PARK RACE TRACK." We sputtered to a stop in the narrow parking space beside the fence, piled out of the car and went in while Dad got a bucket of water and poured it into the radiator. It was quite a while before we started again. The owner wasn't particularly busy at the time so Dad chatted with him until the motor had cooled down.

When we got back into the car, we seemed to be heading toward the clouds on the steep winding road ahead of us. It was narrow with unmarked lanes and we worried that we might meet another car as we swerved out or in too far on one of the curves. (That says something about the density of the traffic at that time.) Although we couldn't tell by looking, we knew when we had reached the top. We could almost feel the car sigh with relief when it ceased to struggle.

Then began the downhill!

Almost as if it had taken a second wind, the car rolled forward, gradually at first, and then with increasing speed. The roller coaster had again sprung to life. Dad's eyes grew big and the knuckles on his hands were paper white as he gripped the steering wheel. The car careened down the roadway and around the curves, leaning far to the right over the empty roadside. We could see the ground far, far below. The car tilted dangerously at every sharp curve. It was built rigid and upright, narrow and high, and the center of gravity was so far off the ground that it tilted, even at twenty or thirty miles an hour. Mother sat stiffly, as she held on to the door handle. Her face was pale and her lips hard-compressed. She didn't say anything, but every once in a while we would hear a hissing intake of breath. Grandmother sat stolidly, apparently calm and composed, keeping whatever alarm she may have felt to herself. We young ones were apprehensive but quiet.

I was half-thrilled by the speed and the movement of the car and half-frightened by the tension that Mother and Dad were exhibiting. The tires were squealing and the brakes were squawking at every turn. Dad's hold on the wheel was so tight that he turned too stiffly and the car jerked a little too far to the right and then a little too far to the left. Sometimes it rode on two wheels. Dad braked furiously at each turn as we swayed down one hill and up another only to start another tumultuous descent. We could smell the hot metal of the complaining brakes but there was no place to stop. I don't know how many miles of this there were but it seemed endless. As dusk approached, the road evened out as it passed rolling pastureland and cornfields.

We were nearing Terre Haute, the largest town we had seen since we left home. The city streets were broad and U.S. 41 went right through the center. It passed by the County Court House, a huge granite structure with a dome impressive enough to be a state capitol. It dominated the town. A statue in memory of Northern Civil War Soldiers was on one corner of the grounds and one representing a World War I doughboy was on another. We had frequent stops at traffic lights and many twists and turns as the highway went by residential areas, business sections, past the Clabber Girl Baking Powder factory and finally past the smelly slaughter house of the meat packing factory. I couldn't imagine how the residents who lived nearby could stand it.

On the outskirts at the south side of town there was a

row of cabins with a sign "CUM BAK INN." It was a tourist camp, many of which had sprung up along the roadside between towns, to accommodate traveling families. Businessmen and more affluent travelers stayed in the hotels in town, but growing families such as ours, struggling to get ahead, found it more economical to "camp" along the way.

There were several separate little white cabins, approximately ten feet square, with high peaked roofs standing about ten feet apart. It was good to get out and run around the grounds while Dad arranged for our stay. Soon we were called back to carry our things from the car to the cabin. Ours was the fourth or fifth one from the gas station that served as an office.

Off to one side was a wooded area, a pair of wooden outhouses, and some picnic tables. After we took the suitcases into the room, Mother and Grandmother set out our evening meal. They used the picnic table nearest a covered shed that provided shelter for a sink and a two-burner gas plate that was fed from a meter in twenty-five-cent amounts. This time we may have had cold fried chicken, pork and beans, sliced tomatoes, hot coffee, and cold milk (bought at the gas station). Mother made the coffee and heated water to wash the dishes there.

By the time everything was put away, darkness had come. A dim bulb on a pole opposite the center of the cabins gave enough light for us to see to move around. A single bulb hanging down on a cord lighted the little cabin. Mother, Grandmother, Bill, and I stayed there. Dad and Jim slept on the front and back seats of the car.

The bed where Mother and Grandmother slept had link wire springs, like those on a rollaway bed, under a flat cotton felt mattress. The sheets were clean. The one little chest of drawers was new and shiny and a cotton throw rug lay flat on the floor. It had been a long day for us and Bill and I fell asleep on an army cot with a thin cotton mattress, his head at one end and mine at the other.

The next morning the first question was, "How did you sleep?" Jim and Dad claimed to have done very well in the car. Dad did get up about midnight and move to the top of one of the picnic tables so he could stretch out. Mother and Grandmother had slept well. No one asked about Bill and me. Apparently refreshed, we were ready for our second day of travel.

We started the day with a good breakfast since Mother could cook and supplies were available from the store in the gas station. While we were eating, Jim called our attention to a whine he could hear. We all got quiet so we could listen. The whine was high and thin much like a giant mosquito. It came closer and became louder until with a loud—whoosh—a white sport car with the top down passed us, tires whining, on out to the distance.

"Why that fellow must be going sixty miles an hour!" Dad exclaimed. "No one needs to go that fast. What if he meets another car on a curve?"

We finished our breakfast in high dudgeon and no other cars, fast or slow, passed us until we got back on the road.

There were numerous barns with high-pitched roofs in view of the highway. From the tops of many of them we were told to chew "Mail Pouch" or "Red Man" tobacco. On the weathered boards of the sides we often saw painted signs which urged us to smoke "Lucky Strike" or "Camels." For those who rolled their own, there was "Bull Durham." These signs, now considered unsightly and illegal near the highway, provided us with diversion during the long ride. They also, in all probability, paid the farmers' taxes.

There were billboards advertising "Wonder Bread" and "Gold Medal" flour. Others were pushing "Model" cigars. "Did you say ten cents?" "Yes, I said ten cents," the ad would say. On the ads for "Dutchmasters" cigars, there were Pilgrims as big as life, but no mention of price. The sign saying "Smoke Murials, a fine Cigar" amused me. I had a friend named Muriel.

Wrigley's Spearmint Gum signs were numerous. Along the corn fields interrupting the Burma Shave jingles were little tin signs advertising "Pioneer Seed Corn" or "Keystone" wire fences. John Deere and McCormick tractor ads dueled from opposite sides of the highway. Quaker State and Penzoil products were also touted. We saw the advertisements for new autos, Ford, Chevrolet, Studebaker, La Salle, Packard, Buick, Essex, Hudson, and so on.

Almost any time someone in the car mentioned that they were afraid something would happen, such as a broken radiator hose or a flat tire, or even a broken axle, it did. In our family it was considered bad luck to say anything about the tire ads such as Goodyear-Silvertown, Firestone, and Siberling. We saw the signs but didn't discuss them.

By noon we were on the outskirts of Vincennes. A pleasant wooded area where we could drive off the road, spread our picnic things, and "stretch our legs," came into view. We had cold sandwiches and pop again.

In addition to the corn and hay fields there were huge patches of watermelons, cantaloupes, and pumpkins along the road. Apple and peach orchards became more plentiful. Large sheds where the local farmers sold their produce appeared on the roadsides. Dad and Mother would exclaim over the beauty of the tomatoes and peppers, the deep green of the pole and bunch beans, the probable freshness and sweetness of the corn, and wish they could stop and get some. However, there was no room in the car and there would be plenty of vegetables of prodigious quality when we got "There."

Soon we reached the bumpy brick and cobblestoned

streets of Vincennes itself. After an abrupt turn to the right, we saw the mound of baled hay, as tall as a three-story building and a block long, close to the stockyard and the railroad tracks on our right. We passed this spot for years and years and the mound never seemed to age or grow smaller. Then there were the sheds and pens for animals: horses, cows, sheep, pigs, goats, and mules that were shipped and received from that siding.

We had left the paved road for a brick-lined street when we entered the town, but we hit the cobblestones when we began to pass the old houses, many of ancient brick. When Mother talked, the jostling movement of the car made her voice warble. She spoke of William Henry Harrison living here when he was the governor and it was the capital of the old Indiana Territory. She mentioned that he made many treaties with the Indians. Later he became President of the United States. Dad came in with the importance of George Rogers Clark, the Kentuckian, who took the town from the English during the Revolutionary War. At that time most of what they were saying went over my head. However, Jim was ahead of me in school and it was a living history lesson for him. (Unless the rough cobblestones shook the information out of his head as fast as it went into it.)

Dad told us that Vincennes had been a seat of learning since the Jesuit priests, who came with French trappers, set up a school before the English, and then the Americans, overran the area. He said, "Vincennes University was started in 1826 and is still an effective college." We didn't go off our route to see it. We had to keep on our way.

The cobblestones ran out and the paving began. The street came to a dead end at the entrance of the largest cemetery I had ever seen. We turned left there and for a long time we glimpsed impressive monuments and tall upright stones that showed above the brick wall that separated them from the highway.

Not long after that we crossed the White River on a beautiful cement bridge with ornamental pillars holding the top railing (just level with our eyes).

Mother had been pleased at our progress toward Princeton, Indiana, where we would get out while Dad checked the gas. However, there rose a barricade across the road. A huge red sign with a black arrow pointing east leaned on the barricade. Another sign just above it announced, "DETOUR."

We turned east onto a narrow gravel road running between two fields of corn. It was obviously just a local road that the farmers used. The gravel at that point was small and the car crunched along smoothly, but after about twenty yards the smooth gravel ran out and we began to bump and bounce over big rocks and jolt down into huge sunken holes in the dirt road that ran between cornfields. Abrupt right turns and then abrupt left turns marked the edges of the farmers' fields. Fortunately, these farmers had huge crops and each field was so large that there were long distances between turns. The corn was high and ran so close to the road that Dad couldn't see what might be coming from the other direction so he slowed almost to a stop at each turn. As we were tossed about in the car Dad told us the current story about this kind of road. It was usually told with a Swedish, German, or Italian brogue. Dad just told it straight.

It seems that there was a man in a tavern in central Europe who was describing his recent trip to the United States.

Someone said, "You drove to all those places? What were the roads like?"

The traveler replied, "Well now, there was some engineer

named Washington who built a good highway from Maine to Florida. It was a wide cement road with signs along the side to tell you how fast to drive and where the curves would be. They even named the next towns. This road was called the Washington Highway."

"There was another engineer that built a good road that went from East to West. He was a good builder, too. His road was called the Lincoln Highway."

"But there were a lot of short roads; the worst roads you ever saw. If they were paved they were full of potholes. Most of the time they were rough dirt or gravel and the only signs said "SLOW" or pointed one way or another. You never knew where you were either!"

"Well, who built those roads?"

"Some fool of a Frenchman named DE TOUR."

We jolted back onto U.S. 41 somewhere between Patoka and Princeton none too soon because the whole family needed to use the bathroom. We found a gas station at the edge of Princeton where Dad gassed up the car and we took advantage of the facilities.

The rest of the way to Evansville was uneventful and we repeated our singing, reading the Burma Shave ads and noting other billboards and points of interest much as we had done the day before.

About sundown Dad spotted another tourist camp and drove into its parking lot. It was on a low slope back off the highway. Only the sign and the roofs of the buildings had been visible from the highway. The accommodations were much like those of the night before. However, they had a restaurant! It was a big building with a curved roof like an airplane hangar filled with long rows of empty tables covered with checkered cloth. We were surprised to see only a few people way over at the other end of the room near the kitchen. We ate our dinner there. Dad commented, "It must be a gathering place for local people on weekends. No restaurant can survive with this small number of customers."

At breakfast the next morning the place was humming with business. I was allowed to have a pancake with syrup. It was probably part of Mother's or Dad's order but it seemed great to me.

To reach the ferry landing where we would cross the Ohio River we had to make our way through the early morning traffic. Evansville was a large town and an important river landing. We passed a number of factories and stockyards. At one point there were huge stacks of great round logs, some of them three or four feet across, beside the street. Dad said they were oak, maple, and other hardwoods. A huge sign near the entrance gate named a manufacturer of fine wood veneers for furniture.

On the south side of town the roadway was built up into a ridge several feet above the ground level. Weeds, trees, and underbrush extended great distances on each side of the road. Beyond them mud and water was all we could see. The car bumped and swayed down a rough and fairly steep bank to the ferry landing.

The river had fallen several feet during the night, leaving a slick muddy area for the cars to cross. Big wooden boards, probably two by tens, were laid across the mud from the solid ground to the edge of the water. There was no real dock. The ferry would come as close to the bank as it could and let down a platform for the cars to drive across.

We watched the boat coming from the other side. It looked like a long, flat barge much like a floating island sticking up about four feet above the water. A huge paddle wheel at the back end propelled it through the water. The wheel must have been about ten feet in diameter with broad blades at the end of each "spoke." The blades dipped into the water and rose and fell much like a broad mill wheel.

The ferry made a gentle arc downstream and then came upstream to the landing.

Several cars were ahead of us on the narrow, muddy lane. We watched as they cautiously eased onto the platform and onto the flat surface of the ferry before we got on. The ferry was two or three cars wide and the first two cars sat right at the edge of the front end of the boat. I wondered if anyone ever drove off into the water. There was a chain across the front but it didn't look as if it would stop anything from rolling off.

All but Grandma got out of the car to watch as we crossed the river. We held on to the railings at the side and looked down at the dark and muddy water. We walked to the back to watch the paddles but the pilothouse was in front of them. All we could do was listen to the chugging engine and hear the slap of the paddles as they hit the river's surface, and the splash of the water dripping off the blades as they rose again. A huge white wake of churning foam followed us. Our path took us in an arc upstream so we could see the other ferry's paddlewheel and its wake better than we could our own. Their path made an arc downstream and then upstream to the landing.

The river was broad, the largest one we had crossed. The bank on the other side was steep and high. To me, the lane going up to the top of it looked like a slick shiny ribbon.

We had been about the sixth car to get on, but we were about the third car to get off. Somehow going across the lowered platform onto the corduroy road in Kentucky wasn't as frightening as it had been getting on from the Indiana side. Although the bank seemed steeper, the roadway was more solid and had a gravel base. We had to wait until the car ahead of us had gone quite far up the bank before we started. One had to keep a safe distance behind the car in front in case it stalled and started to roll back.

That really was an easy crossing. Years later when we were going to see Grandmother Dycus in Metropolis, Illinois, we crossed the Ohio River near Paducah, Kentucky. It had been an extremely dry summer all over the country and the river was exceptionally low. The riverbank going up into the town was frighteningly steep. A huge heavily loaded truck was to drive off the ferry ahead of us. We were the car behind and watched with apprehension as it struggled up the bank. Stakes, about as big around as telephone poles, were driven into the ground to form two parallel rows nine or ten feet apart. They stood nearly two feet high at three-foot intervals all the way to the top of the bank. Two big black men with massive muscles held a big chain attached to each end of a large square beam about the size of a railroad tie and about ten feet long. The truck driver started his engine and drove off the ferry and up the bank about three or four feet. The men hoisted the beam over the first set of stakes and let it drop. The truck's engine stalled and the truck rolled back but it was stopped and held by the big beam braced by the two huge stakes. The driver restarted the engine and after a few feet stalled again. The crossbeam had been hoisted over the next set of stakes and held the truck again. This procedure was repeated over and over until the truck finally reached the top and rolled out onto the street.

Once the truck was safely away, we were signaled to drive off. I had expected us to start up and slide back as the truck had done, but we made it up the bank and out onto the street without stalling even once. Our old Chevy gained a lot of respect from us that day.

The town of Henderson lay at the top of the bank. A beautiful huge oak tree stood in the center of a lovely little park. It shaded a few white chairs and benches on a broad grassy lawn overlooking the river. Across the street from the park was a hotel and a row of stores and business buildings. I would have liked to stay a while. However, Dad had noticed that there were rain clouds to the south and west of us and he felt we should move along. "After all, you got the 'jiggles' out of your legs walking around the deck of the ferry. We had better keep going."

Although it was still early in the morning, the sun was shining brightly, not only on the old Kentucky homes, but on the parched pastures and bare barn lots. It glinted on the surface of the ponds in the fields. It glowed on the new white gravel in the road ahead and shone through the windshield.

A few puffy white clouds like random tufts of cotton glided slowly across the hazy sky. It was pretty to look at but we were getting hot. Mother and Grandmother had begun to fan themselves. Dad occasionally mopped his forehead with his handkerchief. The grimy dust from the road began to cling to our skin. We were glad when we approached a new "black top" area that led into Morganfield.

It was a prosperous town with a large hotel, a number of bright storefronts and offices lining the main street. The new road surface gave off no dust, and the broad street made the town look important.

Expansive lawns, lush and green, sloped upwards to imposing Victorian houses on each side of the road as it led away from the business district. Large trees, predominantly elms and maples, lined the walks. Some trees stood alone and others seemed to frame and shade the houses. We were pointing out various distinctive dwellings as we went along when suddenly we were all jolted and the car began a bump, bump, bump! Dad drove over to the curb and stopped immediately. "I think we've got a flat. I'll check."

Sure enough, "Everybody out," he said. We all piled out of the car and lined up on the walk in front of one of the lovely homes we had admired. Unfortunately, it was one without a shade tree by the road.

Dad began to remove the things that were tied between the spare tire and the back of the car and also the blanket and picnic basket from the floor by our feet. As we piled them up at the edge of the lawn, Mother looked at the cement walkway that rose in easy steps up the long incline to the graciously proportioned bungalow at the top. Then she glanced back down at the ragged pile of our possessions and remarked, "I suppose we would look like bunch of Gypsies getting ready to make camp if someone were looking at us from the house."

Dad and Jim took the back seat out and got out the jack, lug wrench, and the tire iron that were stored under it and began to take the wheel with the spare tire off the back of the car.

Mother, Grandmother, Bill and I were standing, uncomfortably, in the hot sun while we watched Dad and Jim wrestle with the car, when a little lady came bristling down toward us in a crisply starched, smoothly ironed, cotton flowered dress. Her face was creased into anxious lines as she called to us. When she got close enough we could hear her asking, "What are you doing? What's happening?"

Mother introduced herself and Grandmother and explained the situation.

Bill and I were watching Dad under the car setting the jack under the axle just beside the wheel. Jim was putting blocks against the tires at the front and back to keep the car from rolling.

When Mother quit speaking, the lady's face relaxed. She stood there a moment watching and thinking, then said, "It's not good for you and your mother and children to be standing out here in the hot sun. Come up to the house and sit on the porch and wait until they have finished."

We followed her up to the house and stepped into the cool shade of the huge porch and found places to sit among the ladder-back rockers and straight chairs that were there. She went into the house and soon came back with some glasses and a clear pitcher full of lemonade.

While the grown ups talked, I watched Dad and Jim. It was a good thing the spare tire was OK. I thought about how long it would have taken if the tire had to be patched. First they would have had to find the nail (or the source of the hole in the tire), mark the place, then take the tire off the rim with the tire iron. Next they would have to take the innertube out of the tire to find the hole. They would pump a little air into the tube and put it in a tub or bucket of water and watch for air bubbles. If a tub or bucket wasn't handy sometimes they would spit on the spot where they thought the hole was. (It usually bubbled up.) Then they would take out the tire-patch kit and use the little scraper (it looked like a small grater) to rough up the surface of the innertube. There was a little tube of rubber cement that they would squeeze all around the hole and then put the rubber patch on it and hold it until it had dried. Dad would round off the edges of the patch because he said square patches sometimes wouldn't stick well at the corners. Then the inner tube was put back in the tire, and the tire on the rim.

Air was put into the innertube with a manual pump. Dad's first strokes would be fast and easy from his hands and elbows, but as the pressure in the tire built up he would use his whole arms and shoulders and finally whole weight from his hips and waist as well. When his hand-held gauge indicated the correct pressure, about thirty pounds, he would remove the pump and put the tire on the wheel. By the time I had finished thinking of all they would have had to do, Dad had straightened up and had begun to roll the wheel with the flat tire to the front, to be stored on the front fender. Jim was putting tools back under the back seat.

We went down to help put the other things back. Mother thanked the lady for her kindness and we were off again.

At the edge of town the smooth pavement ended, and we mopped and fanned as the car crunched along. The sky became increasingly cloudy and dark and when we reached the edge of Marion, by the big brick house with the slate roof, where we turned south onto a local road, it began to rain a little.

Dad stopped, and we in the back seat stood up and clung over the front while he lifted the back seat up enough for Jim to get out the isinglass curtains and the rods that held them. Jim stuck the rods in their slots. The curtains were really canvas with isinglass panels sewed in to allow the light inside the car while they kept out the rain. They had channels sewn in them that slipped over the rods and big industrial size snaps that fastened them to the roof and back of the car. Dad got pretty wet. The rest of us were sort of damp. Fortunately, it was still warm.

We hadn't gone far when we ran into a wall of rain, a huge downpour. Occasionally a gust of wind would blow some rain in between the fastenings of the curtains, but not much. It was hard for Dad to see. He couldn't use the windshield wiper much because it had to be moved by hand. We crept along for a several miles before the rain lightened up to normal and Dad could watch the road more easily. The rest of us peered through the windshield like Dad because you really couldn't see through the curtains at the sides.

At Fredonia we left the gravel highway and got off on the local dirt road. Nothing can be as slick and unpredictable to travel over as wet, red, Kentucky clay. Horses and mules pulling narrow wagon wheels have trouble staying afoot on the slippery surface and the wagon wheels make deep ruts reaching down to firm ground. Our tires were too wide to make deep ruts, and the motor generated so much horse power that the wheels spun over the surface of the road and the car skidded first to one side and then the other, sometimes going sideways altogether.

There were no ditches along the road at this point so there was no real danger. Dad whirled the steering wheel first this way and then that, trying to counter the skid and keep the car in the center of the road. He was most afraid of getting stuck.

We slithered along for a mile or two, and then we hit a stretch of gravelly road. This was not highway gravel. It was a hilly area where the topsoil had eroded to the gravel beneath; but it was still treacherous since even the gravel was mixed with mud. By now darkness had caught up with us and the headlights on the car bobbled on the road, obscuring and distorting the usual landmarks. When we bounced across a pair of railroad tracks and passed the hazy outline of the big building known as Baker's station, we all cheered. We knew there were only a few more miles to go!

The rain lightened to a drizzle and soon it stopped entirely; but the road remained tricky. The car would lurch forward on gravel and then suddenly slither sideways in mud. Sometimes Dad was able to get into a rut and stay in it, go straight for a while and then unexpectedly skid again.

Finally, at the head of Uncle Billy's lane, we reached the gate. Jim jumped out to open it, and we waited for him after we had driven through. The gate had to be kept locked because cattle were grazing in the field.

The lane was almost a half-mile long, all downhill. Cousin William had imbedded logs across the worst muddy spots, so we went slipping and sliding all the way without getting stuck.

When Dad pulled up at the gate in front of the house he called the usual "Hello," the common practice when approaching a solitary house out in the country, and the rest of us began to pile out of the car. Uncle Billy's family had gone to bed at dark and we had awakened them. They were expecting us, so it wasn't long before Uncle Billy came to the door with a lamp. He was followed by Aunt Nancy and cousins William and Myrtle Mae and old Uncle Bill. We had arrived!

We exchanged kisses and happy, but brief, greetings and made hasty preparations for bed. I got out of my damp clothes, rubbed off with the wash cloth, and holding Myrtle Mae's hand, made an excited rush up the steep stairs to climb onto the huge straw mattress on the high topped bed. I could hardly wait. Tomorrow our vacation would begin!

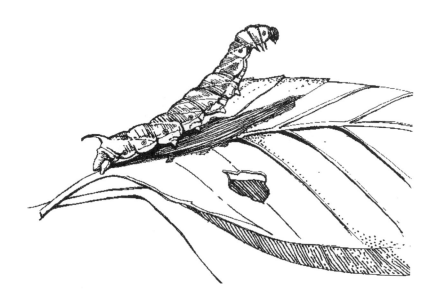

CHAPTER III

Tobacco Worms and Dried Apples

I was happy to share the bed with Myrtle Mae. She was much older than I, a "big girl" whom I much admired. Even though I was tired from the day's travel, I was excited and restless. Myrtle tried to lure me into sleep with all the wiles she knew, such as a whispered "If you lie re-e-el quiet you can hear the fox hunters over on the next farm. . . . Shh, stay still. I can hear them. Listen!"

My high, not so quiet voice, "I don't hear anything. How do you know anyone is hunting tonight? ... What do you hear?"

Her whisper, "Can't you hear the dogs barking way off in the distance?"

"You're just fooling me. I bet there's no one hunting at all."

"Well, do you hear the Katydids? They're insects out in

the trees. Hear them say, 'Katy did. Katy didn't. Katy did. Katy didn't.'"

"Why?"

"Someone said, 'Miller Moller stole a dollar from a chickadee. Katydid ran and hid in an apple tree.' Then the Katydids argued all night long. 'Katy did. Katy didn't.' See if you can count how many times you hear them argue."

. . . "I've counted up to a hundred and they're still arguing!"

From Uncle Billy downstairs, "Myrtle! You two quit talking up there. No one can go to sleep!"

I suddenly realized that Myrtle wasn't making the noise. I was. Crushed, because I had gotten my cousin a scolding, I quieted down afraid to speak again and the next thing I knew it was morning.

Noise in the kitchen woke me up, so I dressed quickly and hastened down the steep stairs. Curious, I scurried through each room as I went. From the clothes and suitcases I could tell where everyone had slept.

As I expected, Jim slept with William Carl. Mother and Grandmother slept in the parlor on the davenport sofa. Unfolded with legs let down, it was a full-sized bed with link springs. When used as a sofa, part folded up to form the back, and part bent down in front. The felt mattress was sewn in sections that allowed it to bend to form the sofa or fold together to form a bed. I think Dad and Billy slept in the parlor on a pallet on the floor. Pallets were usually made of several layers of quilts on the floor with sheets on top. Theirs had not yet been taken up. Sometimes a pallet was made with a feather tick. Once when we were visiting my aunt in Paducah, she made a pallet with a feather tick. It was all fluffed up and looked so soft and inviting that Billy and I belly flopped on it. The feathers flew from under our weight. I bumped my knees and my chin. Billy hit his elbows and his nose. Both of us needed comforting from our shock as well as our bruises. Dad told us of a night when he was young. He and his brother Flaud had to give up their bed to visiting adults so they slept on a feather bed on the floor. In the middle of the night Flaud punched Dad and said, "Hey, Jim. Roll over. It's my turn to sleep on the feathers."

Uncle Billy and William Carl were down at the barn feeding the team and turning the sheep into a new pasture. I think Jim and Dad were with them. Myrtle Mae had done the milking. Aunt Nancy had biscuits made, and bacon and eggs frying. Grandma, helping set the table, was putting out jars of jelly and sorghum molasses. Mother was dressing Billy. I had scrambled into my overalls myself.

There were ten of us for breakfast, Uncle Billy and Aunt Nancy, William Carl and Myrtle Mae, Grandmother Bell, Dad and Mom, Jim, Billy, and me.

There were two large pressed glass pitchers of milk on the table. One held buttermilk and the other held sweet milk. Myrtle Mae had just brought in the sweet milk fresh from the cow. It had been strained through a cloth but was still warm and foamy. Billy was three years old and I was nearly five. We wouldn't drink it. All Mother's persuasion couldn't change us. Jim was older and didn't say anything, but Mother put all our milk aside and let us drink water. However, the milk glasses were put in the cellar, a bricked-in area under the house that was fairly cool and damp. Anything that was to be kept cool was put there. We drank our milk at noon — by then it was not so warm. From then on we drank milk from one milking away.

We enjoyed our breakfast. Sorghum molasses mixed well with butter and spread on hot biscuits was especially good. Of course the sorghum dripped everywhere. It got on our chins, fingers, arms, and elbows—clothes too. There was always a messy cleanup later. Sometimes, William would have been to the pond and brought in enough frog legs for breakfast. M-mm, they were as good as fried chicken—and all white meat.

Dad usually stayed a day or two with us and then went in to Kuttawa. He walked to the road and someone would stop and take him the rest of the way in a wagon or buggy. The roads were so bad in the "bend of the river" where he grew up that he didn't try to take the car. We didn't go with him because we couldn't walk as far as he would have to. He always came back overjoyed at the visits he had had with the friends and relatives that he was able to see.

Mother and Dad and Jim, and when we were old enough, Bill and I, would take part in the work that was being done. It was one way to get to talk to Uncle Billy. He stayed so busy. Once, when Mother and Grandmother were doing some canning with Aunt Nancy, Myrtle Mae, Billy, and I went out in the tobacco patch with Uncle Billy, William, and Jim. They were worming tobacco. At that time the only really effective way to kill the worms was to snap their heads off with your fingers. It was a distasteful job by any standards, but back then "you had to do what you had to do." I squashed the heads of the little and middle-sized ones, but when it came to the big ones I would call for Myrtle Mae. One year we also brought Dick and Marge Prest, who were living with us in Hammond. When Dick found out what we were going to do, he went out to the car and got Dad's pliers. When asked what he would do with the pliers, he said, "Kill the worms! You don't think I'm going to get my hands messed up with those worms do you?"

Just walking through the tobacco was messy enough. The leaves were velvety soft on the surface and clung to you as you brushed by them and handled them looking for worms. Each leaf and stem had to be examined. If a leaf were broken, a sticky ooze got on your arms and on your clothes. The worms, much like tomato hornworms, were ugly and the big ones were fierce looking. Hands became sticky from the tobacco leaves and slimy and greenish brown from the worms.

When we went in for noon dinner, I felt that we'd never get our hands clean even with the lye soap out on the back porch by the wash pans.

Myrtle Mae hastened to get water from the cistern so we wouldn't get the mess from our hands on the rope or the bucket.

The cistern, which lay just outside the side porch, was bricked up to about two feet above ground, and covered with a wooden platform rounded to fit the top. Fastened to the platform was a square box-like structure, approximately three feet high, with a wooden lid. The water bucket, a galvanized heavy pail, rested on the lid. A rope tied to the bucket ran over a pulley hanging over the cistern. The other end of the rope was tied to a heavy piece of chain that held the rope down at rest beside the bucket when it wasn't in use. The pulley was suspended from the end of a two-by-four that had been nailed to a couple of beams on the porch. I can still hear the squeak of the pulley as Myrtle Mae tossed the bucket into the cistern and the scre-e-e-ch it made while the bucket, heavy with water, was slowly drawn up. She filled a couple of wash-pans and put some cloths over the porch rail for us to use when drying our hands.

There was no time to stand on ceremony. We gathered around the wash pans two or three at a time and then dried our hands on the old but clean flour sacks. Warm water and good towels would be used before bed at night.

I doubt if I could make myself worm tobacco today. Fortunately there are effective poisons now.

Most of the time we just followed someone about,

watching whatever was being done or amusing ourselves at whatever came to hand. Almost every day Aunt Nancy and Myrtle Mae, Mother, Grandmother, Billy, and I went into the orchard to pick up apples. They sat on the front porch to peel and core the apples and cut them into sections to be ready to dry. Grandmother's fingers were so knobby she had to quit the peeling soon. Mother noticed her put the knife down. Taking a bone-handled spoon from her apron pocket, she cut an apple in half and handed the apple and the spoon to Grandmother. Smiling her thanks, Grandmother began to scrape the apple between the skin and the core and eat it spoonful by spoonful.

Since Grandmother had no teeth and no false teeth either, all her food had to be soft or chopped up fine. There were no dentists in the area when she was growing up. If a tooth ached someone would advise, "Put a little bit of tobacco on it and bite down. It will soothe the ache." If the

tobacco ceased to ease the pain, someone would know someone else who would pull the tooth. All Grandmother's teeth were gone even before my mother was born.

When the apples were ready, they were dumped into a flour sack. Myrtle Mae took them upstairs, reached through the window in William's room, spread empty flour sacks on the tin roof over the front porch, and distributed the apple slices over them to dry. She worked through the window because the tin roof was as hot as an iron and would burn her.

While they peeled and talked, Billy and I played on the swing between two oak trees in the front yard, or picked and ate grapes from the vines that ran along the garden fence. Sometimes we chased chickens, but were told to stop when we were caught at it. "It might keep the hens from laying."

Aunt Nancy had one rooster that was a fighter. He would challenge the dog, the cats, and the sheep, when they were just outside the gate, and even Billy and me. I was afraid of him. Once, however, he got after Grandma. He landed on her head and messed up the bun she wore her hair in. He was young enough to be tender so he was among the chickens served up for Sunday dinner that week.

CHAPTER IV

Tiny May

My "special" time of day was in the afternoon when Myrtle Mae and I went to bring in the cows for milking. It usually took a long walk over the fields and through the woods until we found them. Then it took a long time trailing behind them until we got back to the stable.

I admired Myrtle Mae. Since I had no sisters, I looked up to her. Although she was not really pretty, she was attractive. Her dark hair, not quite black, formed a soft frame for her face. Her large blue eyes were alert, and a smile seemed to hover around the corners of her lips. She was tall and large-boned, but well-proportioned. Almost always full of good humor, she teased me or told a story as we walked. Often she sang. If I knew the song, I sang along with her.

When we left the house, if she heard the cowbell, she called them. She used a soaring, soothing call that carried a long distance. "Soo—eee, soo—eee, soo—eee, suck, suck, suck."

On rare occasions the cowbell would jangle a little, then ting occasionally, and then jangle furiously as the cows were going down and then up the banks of the gully behind the orchard. Then we would soon see them ambling up the hill by the fence.

Most of the time we heard no bell, so we began to walk. Myrtle Mae seemed to have an idea about where the cows would be. We would a start off on the shortest route to find them. Often we went up the lane and across the field behind Uncle Eddy's place. At the two sycamore trees that marked the boundary with Grandma's place we paused and listened. I never heard anything but she would nod and say, "Let's go this way." We would go through the gap in the fence by the trees and along a path through the woods to an open field. We usually found them where she expected them to be.

On rare occasions they seemed to hide. We would search and search and call and call but would hear nothing. When we did find them they would be in a succulent patch of new growth that they didn't want to leave.

To get their attention she might say, "Hey! Get along there! — Hoo-wee!" while she brandished a stick or a twig or shook a bush. They would turn one by one and head back along the path they had come. We would follow along behind them urging them on when they lingered to graze again.

At the gully or wash behind the orchard, there was a narrow footbridge that we used. The cattle crossed a little further away where the steep bank had been worn down. Daisy's bell would clank and clang as she clambered down one side and up the other with the others following in single file.

Myrtle Mae and I would pause on the little bridge and look over into the pool of water that was always there even when the wash was dry. Usually there was the dark form of a moccasin snake curled on the rocks at the bottom of the water. She said she felt better when he was there where she could see him. When he wasn't in the pool, she kept a good lookout on the edges of the path as she went on up the hill. She didn't want to run into him on the ground. When I was old enough to go that way alone, I followed the same procedure.

At the barn lot she opened the gate and the cows went in, heading straight to the pond for a drink of water. There was a new heifer calf she had named "Tiny May" standing half hidden by her mother in a small lot beside the barn. Excited, I ran to the fence and darted back and forth trying to get a better look. Myrtle Mae said, "If you stand still, she may come to you."

When I finally did stand quietly, the calf shyly stepped in my direction. Myrtle Mae told me to put my hand through the fence, open my hand, and spread my fingers out. When I did this, the little calf locked her big round eyes on my fingers and moved closer. She took my middle finger into her soft slobbery mouth and began to suck. Her broad rough tongue seemed to hold my finger. She looked at me quizzically as she sucked. Just as I thought my finger would come off, she let go, ran her tongue around the outside of her mouth, and went back to her mother. Since my fingers didn't yield any milk, she had lost interest. After that, I went to pet her every time we went to the barn lot.

When the weather was oppressively hot, Myrtle Mae took her three-legged stool out of the stable and milked the cows outside, but she usually let each of them into her stall and poured some grain or bran into the feeding trough. Then she moved to each stall to do the milking.

She always carried a quart cup from which she dipped water to wash the udder and tits of each cow to get them clean before she started to milk. Cats and kittens came from every corner of the barn and hayloft when Myrtle sat down. Some of them scattered away again when they saw me. The bolder ones stayed a few feet away and mewed until she squirted a stream of milk at them, often squirting directly into their mouths. When she missed and hit their faces or sides, they sat and cleaned themselves, then began mewing again.

We usually sang as she milked, the stream of milk going into the bucket, marking the rhythm of the song. If she was milking outside, she commented on the people she either heard or saw going up or down the dirt road that ran by the far side of Uncle Billy's field between his place and that of his neighbor, Pleas Duncan.

She didn't have to see one Ford Model A Coupe which often rattled along the road. She'd say, "Here comes Jesse Rogers. I guess he's going to see Thelma Cash. He's been going there a lot recently."

We could hear the car all the way to Thelma's house. Sometimes it would come back in a few minutes. Then she would say, "I guess he just wanted to ask her to go with him to the pound supper at Luther Riley's house (or some other neighborhood gathering) this Saturday night."

I wondered if that Ford hadn't rattled up her lane at some time for the same purposes, but she was so matter-of-fact about it I thought if it had, it no longer mattered.

When the milking was done, we let the cows out into the field behind the barn and went back to the house with two two-gallon buckets of milk, the soft, foamy liquid licking the rim of the bucket at every step.

CHAPTER V

Quilts and Fiddlin'

One evening while we were at Uncle Billy's we went to see Aunt Nancy's sister Tila (They called her Teely.) Lamb, her husband, and family, who lived on the next farm back. Billy and I trailed behind the grownups as we walked down the hill by the orchard fence. Mother held our hands when we used the narrow footbridge to cross the little stream between the orchard and the woods on the other side. We swished our feet through the heaps of leaves trapped by underbrush at the side of the path, and raced ahead across a small pasture field to the barbed wire fence that divided Uncle Billy's farm from the Lamb place. After the men and boys climbed over the fence, William Carl found a spot where the wires were a little loose and held them apart until we "girls" all got through. Grandmother was a little heavy and the skirt that she wore was long. Mother had to help push down her back and hold up her skirt so that the barbed wire wouldn't tear either the back of her blouse or the hem of her skirt. Then there was just a sloping field down to the house. The Lamb children met us at the gate and escorted us to their parents on the porch with hearty greetings and laughter.

The adults sat down on waiting chairs still talking and laughing over remembered experiences and local news. In a few minutes Mr. Lamb, Uncle Billy, William, Jim, and the Lamb boys, Leeper, Gilbert, and Edwood excused themselves and went in a group to the edge of the yard. I wondered what they were seeing while they looked at the cattle standing beyond the fence. They talked a bit among themselves and came back to the opposite end of the porch, where they sat down and continued talking.

Mrs. Lamb brought out a new quilt she was piecing and had her daughter Dora help her hold it out so we could see the pattern. Mother, Aunt Nancy, and Myrtle Mae admired it and commented on the pattern, color combinations, and the sources of the various triangles and squares of materials. These pieces came from Dora's dress that no

longer fit her. Those came from a dress Aunt Nancy had given her. These other ones were from yard goods bought at Hugh Wake's store, etc.

Billy and I sat nearby too young to be interested in either the men's talk at one end or the women's talk at the other. Mother was continually calling us back to the porch lest we would wander out onto the yard and she was afraid we'd get out of sight and into trouble. Eventually Mr. Lamb brought out some watermelons and cantaloupes and the party became interesting to Bill and me.

When it got dark we all went into the house where Mrs. Lamb lit a kerosene mantle lamp that hung from the ceiling. I think it was the first lamp of that kind I had ever seen. The soft light from above seemed to spread over the whole room leaving no deep shadows. Eventually someone (probably Mom) asked Mr. Lamb to play his fiddle.

After a little pleading he got it out of its aged wooden case and began to tune it up. The case interested me because it was different (almost but not quite square, of dark wood locked with a simple hook) from the shaped case that my violin was in. He held the old instrument against his chest with the scroll resting on his knee. After playing a few hymns and a few songs that Myrtle Mae and Dora requested, he started off on the old jigs and reels that he himself enjoyed. I was fascinated. His bow would bounce on the strings and his fingers raced up and down the fingerboard in impossible rhythmic patterns and with amazing speed. Although he played a number of tunes and called them by name as he played, I can remember only one title, "The Downfall of Paris." When he was younger he used to play at various neighborhood gatherings while the young folk would dance.

By the time we said our good-byes and headed home, the moon had risen. In the hazy light the path was clearly visible and we strung out on it single file because the dew was falling and the grass beside the path was wet. Though it was not quite like walking in the dark, everything was ill-defined. Things seemed to melt into one another as if we were looking through a misty glass. I was looking around in wonder. A fence post, seemingly shadowless, was only a little darker gray than the grass behind it. I drew close to Mother, who was carrying Billy, when we reached the woods. It was dark in there. Mother and Aunt Nancy talked a little louder (for my benefit I guess) while we worked our way through the trees. The men had gone on ahead. Just as we reached the edge of the woods and started to step out into the next meadow, a shrill quivery cry sounded from overhead. A chill went up the back of my spine. My hair must have stood on end and I gave a startled jump and grabbed Mom's skirt.

"Oh, Kakie, that's just a little old screech owl. It makes a scary noise but it won't hurt you. It's just trying to find another screech owl to talk to. Listen! See if another one doesn't call back."

As we walked along I heard another one way far away and then the first one again. This time it wasn't right over my head and I could listen more objectively.

We were just crossing the creek to go up the hill by the orchard when a huge dark figure loomed ahead in the misty light. The field had been clear when we came through it earlier. Again I grabbed Mother's skirt.

This time Myrtle Mae, who was behind me said, "Look at Becky over there sleeping with her head down. I wonder where Mark is?"

Knowing that Becky was their mule and Mark their horse, I was relieved and went the rest of the way up to the house on my own and unafraid.

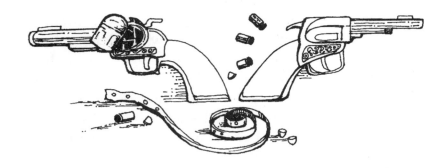

CHAPTER VI

Russell's Blank Pistol

We always spent one day with Mother's childhood friend, Nelly Cash, and her husband and two children. Nelly had lived on the farm next to Mother and the two of them had played together when they were young. Now that they were grown, they liked to remember old times and acquaintances and discuss their growing families.

Just after breakfast we set out walking to Nelly's. We went up the dusty lane from Uncle Billy's to the road, and up the equally dusty road, called the Varmint Trace. It took twenty minutes to a half-hour to get there. By the time we reached the foot of the hill that led up to the house, Nelly, Louise, and Russell were on the front porch waving to us.

Mother and Nelly were very opposite in form and figure. Mother was short and plump. Her cotton figured dress came just below her knees and her bobbed hair was dark with streaks of gray. Nelly was tall and thin, her height accented by her long flowery cotton dress. Her graying blond hair was combed back from her forehead and fastened at the back of her head with a comb. Their mutual affection was apparent. Nelly's smile was warm. Her pale blue eyes glistened and her greeting was happy. Mother's deep brown eyes sparkled and danced as she shouted her opening greetings while we worked our way up the hill.

I looked at Louise with admiration. She was much like her mother, only more vibrant. Her blond hair was curly, probably the result of tight pin curls overnight, and hung almost to her shoulders. Her tall form was covered with a cotton print dress that came just below her knees like Mom's. Her eyes were a deeper blue than her mother's and her broad smile was outlined with lipstick. I guess she was dressed like the girls in town where she went to high school.

Russell seemed pretty tall. He was a little older than Bill and I, but much younger than his sister. He was what they at that time called deaf-and-dumb. Nelly told Mom that when he was about two years old he had a cold and cried and cried no matter what she did for him. He finally got over his cold and quit crying, but she noticed he didn't respond to noises after that. She and her husband took him to the local doctor and then to a specialist in Hopkinsville. Later they went to several other doctors and became convinced that Russell would always be deaf. Since he couldn't hear to learn in the local one-room rural schools, they sent him to a school for the deaf in Danville, Kentucky, during the winter months. He spent the summer months at home. The whole family talked to him with signs, spelling out the words with their fingers.

Nelly and Mother visited on the porch for a few minutes while Russell, Louise, Jim, Bill, and I sat and listened. Louise's fingers darted about explosively as she tried to tell Russell the essence of what was being said. Then Mother and Nelly went into the kitchen to continue their visit while they got dinner ready. Louise was called in to join them.

Russell took Jim and Bill and me out into the yard to see the things he had to play with. We communicated by pantomiming. Large, exaggerated gestures and facial expressions worked most of the time. When all else failed we went to a bare spot in the yard and took a stick and wrote out key words. It worked very well, except that Russell enjoyed correcting my spelling.

By the back steps there was a miniature iron stove just like the one Nelly and Mother and Louise were cooking on. Russell took a tiny bent metal tool and showed us that each of the little stove lids lifted off and that each of the stove doors opened. We found little sticks to put in the firebox and lit them. We gathered grass and clover leaves and boiled them in little iron pots and skillets that were just the right size for the stove. I was fascinated. My toy stove at home was clearly make-believe. However, I wouldn't get burned and I wouldn't set the house afire using it.

Soon we were told to wash up for dinner. Nelly gave the dinner bell a tap, and by the time we were through washing, her husband, Leonard, came in the back gate carrying several ears of field corn. He had shucked and silked them on his way to the house, so Nelly washed them and dumped them into a pot of water that was already boiling on the stove. Soon after everyone was seated, Mr. Leonard said the blessing. Mashed potatoes, fried chicken, squash, mustard greens, biscuits, and the corn were passed for us to eat. Mother declared that no one knew how to pick the ripest and best field corn as well as Leonard. Nelly said that he always managed to bring it at just the right moment when she was cooking. The adults all seemed to enjoy reminiscing and then discussing current affairs. When we had finished the apple (or peach) pie or cobbler, we youngsters were excused from the table to go play again.

This was one of the years Dad's vacation was near the Fourth of July, so Bill and I had our cap pistols with us, They were made of a bright silvery metal and could hold a whole roll of caps and shoot them off rapidly. Until this year our cap pistols had shot only one cap at a time. We used them playing Cowboys and Indians for a while. We'd run behind a tree and peek out and fire at one another. I was usually the Indian so I got to die a lot. We ran out of caps early too.

Finally, Russell went into the house and brought out a pistol that looked like ours, but, where our pistols had a flat plate that the cap laid against when the trigger released the hammer, his had a hole. It wouldn't shoot caps but by then we were just shouting "bang" anyway.

After while he asked his mother for a quarter to go to the store. He didn't say what he planned to buy and she didn't ask when she gave him the coin. We went down the hill at the opposite end of the lot from the path we had used coming to the house. At the fork in the road at the foot of the hill there was a store built on a little rise. Steps went up to a landing at one end and the other end was just high enough off the ground to be level with a wagon bed. On each side of the wide front door in the center of the building there were large glass windows with many small panes through which we could see a long dark counter. High shelves filled with merchandise lined the walls, including the wall behind the counter. This store had been there for years. Mother had said that when she was a girl it was called Woodall's store, and at that time it was also a post office addressed as Poe, Kentucky. Now it was called Duncan's store and was no longer a post office. We entered, and Russell bought a box of twenty-two short bullets. Bill and I were surprised that there weren't any caps, or any fireworks. Mr. Duncan explained that around there they had fireworks only at Christmas. There would be plenty then.

After we went back to the house, Russell took his pocketknife and cut off the lead that stuck out from the copper casing of several bullets. He got Bill and me to pick up some tin cans that were near the house and put them up on a railing under a peach tree that stood by the hen house. Then he stood back about six yards from them and shot his pistol. The lead that was still in the bullets was sufficient to knock the tin cans off the rail. Bill and I were really excited! Russell let each of us try with the pistol but we had little luck. Jim was somewhat better, but could do with a lot of practice.

In a little while Mother called us from the back porch and said it was about time to go. However, as we started to the front of the house, Nelly mentioned that they were going to take down the old stone house that stood about ten yards behind the back porch. It had been their home until they built the wooden house in which we were visiting. Mother asked if they couldn't use the house for some other purpose. Nelly said, "No, the old place was so hot in the summer we could hardly stand it. The stones would hold the heat like a brick oven, and the house didn't cool off at all during the night. In the winter the stones became icy cold and kept the rooms chilly even when there was a big fire in the stove. The fireplace never kept the room warm. When the stove was hot the walls would sweat and moisture would run down to the floor. I'm just glad to be out of it."

Mother said, "Let's go take a last look. You know my older sister and her husband lived here when Tom was working for your dad. I spent my first night away from home in that house."

We all went to look. It was made of common fieldstones

of random shapes and sizes held together with mortar. A steep roof of cedar shakes topped the building, which was a story and a half high. We looked inside. There was only one room about eighteen feet square with high steep steps leading from the far corner to the upstairs. It was dark. Only one window by the front door let the light in. No wonder they were glad to move out.

Many years later I learned that Russell's pistol was made to fire blank bullets. Jim went to the store when Billy and I weren't around and got himself one and some blank bullets, too. When he was home in Hammond he and some of his friends shot it off in the big double garage that belonged to the father of one of the boys. They were excited by the noise it made. However, he ran out of blanks and, not knowing where to get more, he got some twenty-two bullets. When he shot the first one the whole pistol disintegrated in his hand. He was lucky not to get hurt. This is one of the things that Mom and Dad never heard about, neither had I until I asked him about Russell's pistol. Then I got the whole story.

CHAPTER VII

Snakes, Yellow Jackets, and a Gypsy Baby

One day when Myrtle Mae and I came in with the grapes we had picked from the garden fence, Mother said, "Catherine, it looks as if you will be celebrating another birthday at a 'Graveyard Cleaning Off.' Billy just got word that the families with people buried in the Providence Cemetery are going to gather there Wednesday to weed it and fix it up."

As I remember, Uncle Billy hitched up the wagon and put in shovels, garden hoes, grubbing hoes, rakes, pitchforks, axes, sickles, and any other tool that he thought might come in handy. Aunt Nancy and Myrtle Mae put in quilts, towels, a dipper and some empty buckets for getting drinking water, and boxes and baskets of picnic style dinner fixins'. Jim, Bill, and I were the only children going. School was held after the planting season of March, April, and May, and before the harvesting season, which started in September. This was August and the boys and girls our age were in their classes. When everything was ready we got into the wagon and headed out.

Providence Cemetery was located at a level place on the hill just off the left side of the road that led all the way to the town of Kuttawa from the end of Uncle Billy's lane. It wasn't far, so we were the first to arrive. All summer every time we went to town or church we had passed the cemetery scarcely aware of it. This time I looked carefully as we drove.

Over the scraggly roadside growth I could see the three large oaks, spaced at intervals like sentinels, marking the north side of the cemetery. There was a neatly cleared square outlined by a low granite curbing under the first tree. A granite monument about two feet tall and two feet wide stood on a low base at the head. Near the next oak there were a few good-sized fieldstones almost covered by grass and weeds. The modest granite tombstone where Grandpa Bell was buried lay near the base of the third. As we came closer the smaller trees along the west and south became visible, as did the view of the whole cemetery.

Although the area had been cleared the year before, annual and perennial weeds and grass had re-established themselves. Except for the few larger tombstones and some standing slabs, most of the gravesites would have been hard to identify. Strands of barbed wire, put there to keep livestock from straying among the graves, hung in sagging rusty strands from the posts marking the east side. Wires also drooped from the corner post on the southeast to posts and some young trees along the south. They were stapled to one of a clump of sassafras and persimmon trees marking the southwest corner and other young trees on the west. Behind the trees on the west a sunken lane led down to Newt Cash's spring.

A large oak near the east side and another toward the middle of the cemetery gave a restful cool look to the area beneath them. A cluster of tall cedar trees near the west side provided deep shade where little grass and no weeds were growing. Several monoliths like tall granite wafers stood there. Some were erect and some leaned forward or back. One small white column about four feet high stood out in the shadowed plot.

The somber red granite monument of W. W. Duncan dominated the western end of the cemetery. Simple granite markers, about a foot high and a foot-and-a-half wide, and fieldstones, some of them limestone, and some of them clay-colored conglomerates about the size of the markers, lay among the grass, briars, and other noxious vegetation dotting the grounds. Granite tombstones stained by mildew and moss, although taller, fared little better. This locality had been a pioneer community hacked out of the wilderness by those who were buried here. The fieldstones and the tombstones seemed to be struggling to be seen amid the onslaught of weeds, bushes, wind and rain, much as those whose places they marked had struggled to live against the same and other hazards.

Before any of us could get out of the wagon, other families began to arrive. They stepped to the ground with much laughter and hearty affectionate greetings. Usually the men grabbed their tools and went straight to work. I suppose they didn't feel a need to socialize since they often shared work in the fields during the week or met when getting supplies in town. The women, who had not seen each other except occasionally in church, took a lot of time to talk while they gathered the things they would use. Then, too, they may have felt that the men, by creating a disturbance in the weeds and grasses when they entered the area, might cause the "venomous varmints" to slither away before they began their own cutting and hacking.

Wielding their grubbing hoes and shovels, the men began to dig up the bushes and stubborn weeds. Some of them started re-setting fence posts and shoring up the sagging wires; others chopped up fallen branches and sawed dead limbs from the trees. The women scraped off the unwanted grass and bamboo briars with the sickles and garden hoes. Jim, Bill, and I "fetched and carried."

I was surprised at the jovial mood that prevailed in spite of the place in which we were working. The day was hot; the work was hard; the shirts of the men and the dresses of the women were soon wet through and sticking to their backs and arms. The towels used to mop sweating brows became dirty and wet, but the friendly banter and the tall tales did not cease; neither did their labor.

Occasionally a startled shriek would rise from among the stones, when a toad would jump up from the grass in front of one of the ladies. Once a monstrous squeal arose from the women working in the weeds at the western edge by the lane. "Kill it! Kill it! Somebody come quick!" sounded from several women at once.

Some of the men, probably the husbands of those upset, ran over with a grubbing hoe or ax to help. Among the comments of, "Oh. it's just a puff adder, ...Won't hurt no one." "It's just an old hog nosed snake. Let it be." The screaming went on until someone severed the body of the snake and tossed it into the adjoining pasture for the buzzards to get later.

One time a gruff shout was heard and several men darted away from a corner spot batting and waving their arms and uttering indistinguishable guttural exclamations. Careful not to curse in the presence of the ladies, they turned and ducked and bobbed their heads. One of the men went around to several groups of the women and explained that they'd come upon a nest of bumblebees or yellow jackets, and it would be wise for the women to avoid that area today. "This evenin' Pleas Duncan will come back and pour 'coal oil' down the hole to get rid of 'em," he added.

When the disturbance died down, their work resumed.

From time to time someone who was "resting" went down the hill to Newt Cash's spring for water. Jim and Bill usually went along with one or two of the men. When Myrtle Mae, Isabel Arnold, Lucille Duncan, and Louise Cash went, I just tagged along. The bucket was too heavy for me to carry. Sometimes we'd wander into a thicket of bushes out of sight of the cemetery to take care of physical necessities before we went to the spring.

I watched as mother carefully pulled weeds and grabbled grass away from the base of Grandpa's tombstone. She was quiet and reflective. Feeling that she might rather be let alone, I left her and wandered about looking at the graves. At the east end of the cemetery I noticed three very small tombstones. Little lambs carved at the top peeked out from the weeds. I separated the growth to read the inscriptions. The birth and death dates on each stone were so close together they had to be babies that didn't live long. The death dates on the stones, too, were only a year or so apart. Such a sad thing.

When the women finished clearing the area where their own families lay, they tackled the weeds along the fences or cleaned around the graves of those who no longer had family members in the area. I noticed Ethel Riley on her knees rubbing an old dry scrub brush across the mildew on the last of a cluster of white slabs between the cedars and the western fence. Apparently she felt she had finished there, for she straightened her tall form, dusted off her skirt, stretched and twisted, and rubbed her back a little. Tossing the scrub brush into her tool basket, she glanced at a group working along the fence at the south side. She picked up her hoe and basket and walked over to join them saying, "You're almost down to the spot where the little Gypsy baby is buried."

"What?" someone exclaimed!

"Yes, the Gypsy baby. It is buried right over there by the fence."

"I never heard of any such thing!"

"Well, it's true. One night years ago, a Gypsy family came through here. The woman had gone into labor so they stopped at a clearing in the cemetery until she had the baby. The poor thing died." After a pause, pointing about midway along the fence, she continued, "They buried it right there. You never know about Gypsies. They drove off the next day and no one has ever seen or heard of them since."

She stopped and thought a moment. Then she said, "I can't remember who it was but someone stopped here, and one of the Gypsies explained the situation and showed him the place where the baby was buried. He told my father about it a long time after they had gone."

In thoughtful silence the women went back to hacking at the weeds, each musing about what she had heard. By the time they finished the fence row, however, they were chatting again.

I wandered over to the spot that Ethel had left and looked down at the white stones lying flat on the ground. Grieving hands had scratched the identity of those who rested there into the surface with some sharp farm tool in years gone by. Already the names and dates were growing dim. The soft limestone was succumbing to the effects of wind and rain.

Across Newt Cash's lane there was a little clearing where

he had made some "new ground" for his plant bed in the spring. It had grown up in weeds but he had mowed it so it would be smooth for those working there that day. About noon the women went to the clearing and began to lay out the picnic dinner. To me this was almost as good as camp meeting. Chicken, ham and biscuits, ripe tomatoes both red and yellow, sliced cucumbers, potato salad, bean salad, and cakes and pies were spread out on the tablecloths over the quilts on the ground. Fresh buckets of spring water were placed at one edge of the tablecloths. The most senior man led the blessing before we began to eat.

While the plates were being filled, Mother said, "Today is Catherine's birthday." Several of the women smiled and asked how old I was, but no big fuss was made over it. Birthdays were not big events in the families there. It was all right with me. I eyed Ethel Riley's three-layer coconut cake, Mrs. Gus Duncan's sunshine cake, and Allie Ennis' chocolate cake, but I loaded my plate with a piece each of Isabelle's chocolate pie, Lucille's or Aunt Linnie's apple pie, Nelly Cash's peach cobbler, and Myrtle Mae's blackberry pie. Mother didn't notice that I had done only lip service to the chicken, potato salad, biscuits, and tomatoes.

The men went back into the graveyard and loaded the limbs, bushes and other large growth onto someone's wagon, possibly Bob Riley's or Harry Cook's, to be hauled off and dumped into a gully somewhere on his farm. In the southwest corner there was a small pile of dirt, left after graves were dug. Grass and small debris was raked over there to rot away during the fall and winter.

When the tools were all put back into the wagons we turned to look back. The scene had changed. The barbed wire hung taut and straight on all three sides and the ground under them was smooth and weedless. Whether they were granite or fieldstones, the headstones and footstones were clearly identifiable and stood facing east in irregular rows. The tall thin monoliths rose from the ground, more prominently erect or askew. Other stones standing on granite pediments were scattered throughout the cemetery. Several identical stones in a neat row marked graves of a single family whose losses had come close together. There were double monuments that denoted husband and wife. Some of the monoliths had broken off and lay flat over the grave like the limestone slabs in the corner. The little lambs on the stones in the east corner were now clearly visible. There were no flowery inscriptions on any of the tombstones that I remember. Fieldstones were the most prevalent markers.

After the women were through putting away the picnic things, various couples and families walked among the gravestones meditating on those who lay buried there. Except for Grandfather's monument, most of the rest of the graves in our family's area were marked with the simple fieldstones. They were large hunks of reddish, clay-like rock, probably a combination of jasper, agate, iron, and flint, which underlay most of the soil in this district.

Mother would stop at each of these primitive markers and speak of the person buried there. We stood by a small granite stone with "Sintha Blake" engraved on it. "This is where Mother's Mother is buried. When I was a little girl she couldn't do much but sit by the fireplace and smoke her pipe. Sometimes, when her pipe went out, I would fill it and take up one of the coals from the fireplace to light it for her."

I didn't think to ask how she handled the coals without getting burned, but there must have been a way.

A couple of stones away she commented, "Hanna Bazore, that was Daddy's sister, is buried here. When her husband died she came to live with us. It looks as if the grave has sunk a little. I'll mention it to Billy." Uncle Billy was good about taking care of things for the family.

Then there was the little marker for Phebe Blake. "Poor Phebe," she said, "She had a hard life when she was young, and was never healthy. Only a few years after she married Uncle Bill she died. He says the happiest years of his life were those when they were married."

"Here is Sister Susie. Her husband was Tom Winters. The first night I spent away from home I stayed with them. They were living in that old stone house behind Nelly and Leonard Cash's place."

Mother had spoken of each person with love and affection. Somehow I, too, felt a warmth toward them. Here was my great grandmother and my grandaunt, grandfather, and others. Family gone by.

We roamed through the rest of the cemetery stopping for comments about and memories of neighbors and friends.

Soon everyone drifted back toward the wagons. The men exchanged a few comments, nodding at the sunken graves and the yellow jacket nest, and seemed to reach an agreement before driving off.

The cleaning day was over but the work was not quite done. The next day Uncle Billy got a wagonload of dirt from somewhere on his farm to take to the cemetery. With Billy and me in the wagon he drove over the whole place shoveling dirt into each sunken grave and jumping down off the wagon to smooth it off with a rake. Billy and I tried to help but the rakes were too heavy and, after a few tries, we stayed in the wagon.

When he had finished with most of the graves on the south side of the cemetery he took the team over to the southeast corner. I didn't see any markers or sunken spots so I asked why we were going there.

"You see where it looks like the soil is washing away.

Well, I been told that there's a family buried there. Strangers, … said they were aimin' t' go out West…. Sort-a livin' outen' their wagon and jes' stoppin' by the side of the road at evenin'. They prob'ly stopped back there by Brewster Creek where the water was handy. Anyway, they told somebody passin' by that one of 'em took sick in the night and they couldn't go on. The next day another was sick. They didn't ask fer help. One day somebody come by and found 'em all dead.

"The horses were found staked a little way off. The grass around 'em was eaten plumb down and their water buckets was bone dry. The wagon and all was so fouled up that the feller who found them thought the family must a had cholera. He got some people to help burn the wagon 'n things. Someone took the team off to a field away from other stock 'til he was sure they were all right. The bodies were brought here and buried all together. I just don't want the land to wash away at this corner."

Once, while Uncle Billy was smoothing off a grave beside the wagon, I was standing at the front watching him. A horsefly or something disturbed the mule and she made a sudden move and joggled the wagon. I fell pell-mell right under her heels. In a moment Uncle Billy was there steadying the mule and bending over to pull me out.

"Good heavens! It's a wonder she didn't kick you. She's usually skittish. She could a killed you!" He didn't scold. He was just concerned and grateful that I wasn't hurt.

"When you're standin' in a wagon, keep your knees bent a little. They'll act somethin' like a spring and let you stay up when thay's a rough spot in the road or the team makes a sudden move like old Beck did just then."

I took Uncle Billy's comments to heart and still remember to bend my knees when standing up in a moving vehicle.

He went back and finished that grave and all the others. As we left, he commented, "This fall after a good rain, I'll come up with some new seed and put it on the places that I've just filled. By winter there should be a good covering of grass."

CHAPTER VIII

Poor Huntin' and a Nervy Squirrel

There were three guns in the kitchen at Uncle Billy's. One, about the size of the BB gun Jim had at home, was mounted over the door leading to the front room. The other two, a twenty-two rifle and a double-barreled shotgun, were mounted on the back wall. William used the guns on the back wall for hunting.

He was a good hunter. I often saw him with his long leisurely stride coming up the hill beside the orchard, his gun cradled in his left hand and a couple of rabbits hanging from a string tied to his belt. He usually took the game out behind the back fence to skin and clean. He'd take a pan of salt water, clean the meaty portions and take them to Aunt Nancy, bury the entrails and unusable parts, and take the pelts into the smokehouse to work on later.

Almost always there were squirrel or rabbit skins

stretched and nailed to the smokehouse wall. I didn't often see bullet holes in them. When I asked him about it, he said, "Have to shoot game in the head. If there are bullet holes in the body I get paid just about half as much as I do for whole skins when I sell them. These pelts here have their summer fur on them. They won't sell, but after they're cured I can use them to patch harness and equipment."

Most of his spending money came from the hunting and trapping he did in winter. The animals had their thickest fur then. Sears and Roebuck and other firms who advertised in the local paper and farm magazines paid good prices for his fox, squirrel, rabbit, and muskrat pelts.

One quiet afternoon William showed us the guns from the kitchen. He brought down the little one first. Instead of being a BB gun it was a small light-weight twenty-two rifle, about twenty-seven inches long weighing three or four pounds. Billy and I took turns while he explained how to hold it and how to line up the V-shaped groove in the gun sight on the near end with the little ball at the far end of the barrel. Even though the gun was empty he told us to treat it as if it were loaded. "You never point a gun at anyone, even if you think it's empty. You don't carry a gun on your shoulder like a soldier on parade. You carry it across your breast so you can move it into a position to shoot in a hurry!"

Bill and I were anxious to try shooting, but he made us wait. He took the rifle he used for hunting from the back wall of the kitchen and let Jim hold it. It was longer and heavier than the one he had shown Billy and me. Since Jim caught on quickly, William showed him how to load it, pointed to a post he could use as a target, and let him shoot. Jim hit the post three shots out of five. Then William showed Billy and me how to load the little rifle. He set a wide plank up against the fence and told us to shoot at it.

Billy went first. He was a boy! We each managed to hit the plank part of the time.

When Dad came out of the house with the Brownie camera to get a picture of us, William went back inside and got his shotgun so each of us would have a gun to hold. Billy held the little rifle, I held the big one, and Jim held the shotgun.

When Dad was done, Billy and I urged William to shoot the shotgun and let us see how big a hole it made. He didn't like to waste ammunition but he consented. Wow! What a noise and what a hole! It must have been three inches wide, and went clear through the plank.

Billy and I wanted to try it but he said we weren't big enough. Even if we could hold the gun, it would knock us over when it fired. He said Jim could try it. Then he showed Jim how to hold the gun tightly against his shoulder so that when he shot, the gun's recoil wouldn't strike him hard enough to make a bad bruise. Jim aimed at the plank and pulled the trigger. He hit the plank all right but he staggered around to keep from falling. Rubbing his shoulder, he handed the gun back to William. He didn't get bruised but he had developed an awesome respect for the shotgun.

One afternoon when William didn't have to work the tobacco, he suggested that Jim could go hunting with him. Billy and I clamored to go too. William talked a little with Mom, then finally said, "Yes, but you'll have to be very quiet. You can't talk and you must stay right behind Jim and me on the path."

Jim didn't complain about our tagging along although I'm sure he was disappointed. We took off up the lane in front of the house and then turned across a pasture field toward the woods on Grandma Bell's place. It was the beginning of squirrel season so William figured the hunting would be good.

The cows had created a path clear of leaves and brush and wide enough for us to walk sometimes two abreast and sometimes single file along the edge of the woods. William led. Jim followed. Bill and I trailed close behind them single file in the rear, each vying to get in front of the other all the while.

William cautioned us not to bump into bushes or step off onto leaves or twigs and not to talk. He led slowly and steadily sweeping his eyes first over the ground and then into the overhanging branches. Pausing under a hickory tree he motioned us to keep still. Then, looking up intently, he raised his rifle and pointed it toward a low branch. Excited, I shrilled out, "What do you see!"

There was a sudden rustling among the leaves and William brought down his gun. "A squirrel was on that second branch right near the trunk, but he got startled and jumped away," he explained softly.

We started walking again. Embarrassed that I had frightened the game, I silently trod behind while Billy sent glaring glances back at me.

I tried to see everything at once, glancing up at the trees and then into the few bushes and high grass along the fence, at the path, and at the bases and trunks of the trees. Suddenly a shiver went all over me and the hair at the back of my neck tingled. There, coiled up between the roots of a large tree, was a snake. Afraid to make a noise again, I announced in a great stage whisper, "There's a snake by that big tree right by the path where we are going."

William kept on walking. In a soft voice he responded, "Unh hunh, I've been watchin' 'im. He's a black snake. Probably sleeping off a good dinner. Just keep walking. Don't speed up or slow down. Pretend you don't see 'im. He won't move if you just keep goin' like you're goin' now."

It was hard to keep my pace. It was hard not to look at

him either. My shoulders and feet faced forward but my head cocked to one side a little and my eyes walled over to his sleek form as we passed him. I was almost on my tiptoes ready to run, but just as William had said, he didn't stir.

Beyond this point the path left the fence and took a turn into the woods. Here it became a trail covered with leaves all trodden down and damp so our footsteps were muffled. It seemed like twilight as the branches of the huge trees intertwined and allowed little light to filter through. There were a few bright spots where a dead tree stood, or an old tree had fallen. Being a little awed by the darkness I was quiet too. We didn't see any sign of squirrels and soon came out at the far side of the woods where we had to climb over a barbed wire fence. William laid his gun on the ground on the other side of the fence and explained, "You never lean your gun on the fence. It might fall and go off while you are not holding it. The bullet could go anywhere." By the time he had quit talking we had all gotten to the other side.

The cows had not made a path here so there were bushes and small saplings to walk around. Eventually we hit a sheep trail that ran along the left side of the woods. I noticed a group of five or six medium-sized trees that surrounded an open space perhaps eight feet square. The ground between them was flat except for a little mound in the center covered with green moss. It was about as long as a man might be tall and shaped as if a man were sleeping on his side with a knee bent. I asked William why that was there.

His response was, "I don't really know. It might be an Indian buried there. They made shallow graves. Years ago they used to camp in these parts when they were huntin'."

"Let's dig it up and see." I said, looking around for a stick.

"No. We don't disturb the dead if that's what it is. Let it

be." William spoke as he kept on walking. Seeing that we were pretty close to the house, he suggested that we stop there for a drink of water.

Billy and I got so busy telling Mom, Aunt Nancy, and Myrtle Mae about our hunt that we didn't notice when Jim and William disappeared. They returned later in the afternoon with four or five squirrels. After William had skinned and cleaned them, Aunt Nancy put them in a pan of salt water to soak overnight saying, "That'll take away the wild taste. We'll have them for breakfast in the morning."

One year Billy and I felt that we were old enough and had practiced with the little gun enough that we should be allowed go hunting by ourselves. It took us a lot of arguing with Mother, and she had a long talk with William and Uncle Billy before she finally consented.

We set off proudly, excited and confident that we would bring back a squirrel or two. Following the same path to Grandmother's woods that we had taken the first time with William and Jim, we listened for sounds in the trees and watched for fresh nut hulls on the path as we walked along. Suddenly I felt something fall onto my shoulder. Fearing it might be a spider I brushed it off and saw a piece of a nut hull hit the ground. About that time another piece bounced off Billy's head and we looked up. The hickory limb directly above us was quivering and soon another bit of trash came down. We backed off so we could see a little better and, sure enough, there was a squirrel. He was busy nibbling on the nut turning it round and round in his paws and dropping little chunks and shavings like sawdust from his teeth. Billy was holding the gun so he took the first shot. The gun cracked! A few twigs fell down on us, but the squirrel still sat there nibbling away. Billy tried another shot and a bit of bark skinned off the tree several feet above the squirrel who stayed right there.

I was jumping up and down for my turn and finally grabbed the gun, took deadly aim and fired. An empty nut hull fell on my head. The squirrel looked down as if he had just noticed us and was throwing things to make us leave. He wasn't at all afraid. I aimed the rifle again but he jumped over to another limb just as I pulled the trigger. We tried to get in a position to shoot again but he always got behind a branch somewhere and we finally gave up. We combed the rest of the woods thoroughly but found no other squirrels and came back to the house disappointed.

In spite of our disappointment we were amused by the squirrel's nerve. That evening we were telling everyone about our efforts and expressing our indignation at the lack of respect the squirrel had shown us when William laughed and started to tell a story.

"It seems that there was this young feller who wanted to go huntin', but his dad didn't want him goin' alone. The feller was persistent. Finally his dad said he could hunt if his grampa, who lived with them, would go too. Everybody else was busy. The grandfather was old and a little feeble. His walk was slow and his hands trembled. The boy really didn't want to have him along, but it was go with Grampa or stay at home. Off they went. Sometime in the middle of the afternoon they came on a squirrel, prob'ly about as fer up the tree as yours was. The boy took aim and shot. The squirrel looked down at them and jumped to another limb. He fired again and missed. The squirrel didn't leave the tree but jumped each time the boy fired. Finally his grandfather said, 'Son, give me the gun afore that fellah leaves the tree.'

"He took the gun, looked up into the tree and pointed. The boy watched the barrel, as it swayed back and forth and round and round in his grandfather's trembly hands. At last there was a shot and the squirrel fell from the tree.

"When they returned home with that lone squirrel, the family began to tease the boy.

"He was all put out and whined, 'I could have shot him, too, if I could aim over all the tree at once like Grampa did!' "

In our hearts Billy and I figured we'd do better the next time, but the time never came again.

CHAPTER IX

Sunday School and Company for Dinner

Everyone was busier than usual one Sunday morning when I got up. Today there was Sunday School at Fairview Methodist Church. Myrtle Mae had already done the milking, William had done his chores, and they were both sitting on stools in the back yard with a bucket of boiling water between them. They were plucking several young chickens that had just been killed. Soggy clumps of feathers were falling from their fast-working hands. Each chicken was held by its legs and plunged into the bucket. After a few moments they took the chickens out and began pulling off the feathers. I could see what they were doing from the kitchen door, but such a foul odor arose each time a chicken was plunged into the bucket I didn't go out to watch.

Mother was helping Aunt Nancy dress those that had been brought in. Cornbread and sorghum molasses had been set out for Billy and me. Everyone else had finished eating breakfast. While we ate, we watched Mother and Aunt Nancy remove the insides of the chicken, take out the gizzard, heart, and liver and cut the rest into frying-size pieces and place them in a pan of salt water to wait until time to be floured and fried.

Pies were already in the oven. A cake had been baked yesterday. Peeled potatoes were in a pan of salt water ready to be boiled and mashed. Lima beans that had been hulled sat in a pot. String beans and corn were in buckets beside the door. They would be strung or husked and silked later. Big red tomatoes, onions, and several large cucumbers lay on a table by the back porch all washed and ready to slice.

By the time I finished breakfast, Myrtle Mae had come into the kitchen and had begun to break biscuits into pieces and place them in a large bowl. She poured a creamy sauce over each layer.

"What's that?" I asked.

"Biscuit bread pudding." She kept at her task until the bowl was full.

Mother, Grandmother, and Aunt Nancy finished what they were doing, washed their hands, and went to clean up. They weren't going to Fairview with us. Uncle Billy and Aunt Nancy sometimes went there when there was "Preachin," but they were Baptists and usually went to New Bethel Church. They let William and Myrtle Mae go to Sunday School at Fairview because it was close. Mother and Grandmother were staying home with them.

Myrtle took a final dash through the house with the good broom. Then she took an old one to sweep off the porches and the yard where the chickens left messes. They would be penned up in the area by the chicken house today and fed corn and scraps. William soon came in from burying the feathers and went to his room to wash and dress. Myrtle Mae and I took wash pans and a pitcher of water upstairs to her room. I heard new voices downstairs and washed and dressed in a hurry so I could go see who it was.

It was Dora, Gilbert, and Edwood Lamb, Myrtle's cousins from the next farm. William was using some barber clippers to trim the hair on Elwood's neck. He had finished with Gilbert. When Elwood flinched and yelled, "Ouch!" William said, "Sorry, I didn't mean to pinch you. These old clippers ain't workin' right. I've ordered a new pair from Sears and Roebuck but they ain't come yet."

Dora sat quietly on the swing under the oak trees and held her shoes in her hand while she waited.

At last Myrtle Mae came down and everyone rose to walk out the gate, up the lane, and down the road to church. The boys looked spiffy, dressed in their clean pants or overalls, shirts, and shoes with their hair neat and all slicked down. Myrtle Mae and Dora had on their best printed cotton dresses, but they walked barefooted and carried their freshly polished white shoes, so the dusty gravelly road wouldn't spoil them. My city-bred feet were in sandals.

When we turned off the road at the bare graveled area in front of the church, the girls stepped off onto a grassy spot under some trees. Each of them leaned against a tree or held onto a bush while she took a cloth handkerchief out of her purse, dusted off her feet, and put on her shoes. Myrtle Mae commented, "If it had been cool I'd have brought my stockings, but it's too sticky to put 'em on today."

While they were busy, I looked at the fair-sized, white clapboard building. About three-fourths of the way back there was an area which curved out toward the north. It had a tall window. The roof was steep and high. A wagon, a buckboard, and a couple of buggies were tethered in a shady grove on the opposite side of the church.

Uncle Herman's Ford crunched over the gravel in front of the church and stopped in a spot at the edge of the shady grove. Lucille Duncan and her brothers Glenwood, Elbert, and Earl began descending from their father's car. Looking very proper in our crisp cotton dresses and clean white shoes, we went over to greet them.

Jessie Rogers drove up behind the wagon and buggies and skidded to a stop in the graveled, dusty roadway. Immersed in a cloud of dust Lucille coughed and muttered, "Showing off for Thelma Cash, and she's not even here yet."

She chuckled a little and glanced at Myrtle Mae, who gave a hearty laugh. "A wasted show this time."

No one seemed to be in a hurry. This was to be Sunday School. Those present were mostly parents with children, Sunday School teachers, and those of "courting" age. On the third Sunday, when the minister would preach at Fairview, most of the adults in the area, even those without children, came to both Sunday School and church.

Mr. Riley opened the big double doors at the front of the church and we followed his family into a huge room. The walls and ceiling were of cream colored tongue-and-grooved wood. Several oil lamps in black metal bracket holders with bright reflectors were mounted high on each side. A long center aisle separated the cream-colored, square-backed, wooden pews. At the end of the rows of pews, an area on each side curved out and widened the room enough to suggest a cross. Tall clear glass windows were centered in the curve and long benches hugged the walls under them. At the front there was a platform with double windows on both the north and south ends. Several pews sat with their backs to the north windows. A lectern was centered at the front, and a few chairs had their backs to the windows on the south.

Several children about my size rushed ahead of us to the benches under the windows, but I stayed with Myrtle May and Lucille, who went to the pews on the platform at the front. We sat and faced the lectern at the middle of the platform. I realized that we were the choir when other girls that liked to sing came up and joined us.

Myrtle May identified Margaret Glasgow and Maude Green for me as they came in and sat with Ethel Riley in the pews on the north side of the center aisle. The rest of the women soon followed them.

Later the men, who had stood around outside for a few minutes, came in and took seats in the pews on the south side of the aisle. Those men who liked to sing joined us on the platform in the choir. My brothers, Jim and Bill, came up with William.

After Mattie Lee Conger took her seat at the piano on the floor beside the platform and the choir, Mr. Glasgow, the Sunday School superintendent, strode to the front and stood behind the lectern.

"It's good to see so many of you here this mornin'. The last few Sundays have been mighty sparse. 'Course I reckon the bad weather we've had lately hasn't helped. Let's start by singin' a few good hymns. Mattie Lee, what'll it be?"

"Let's do 'There's Power in the Blood,' page 24."

She played about two lines and then went back to the beginning and the choir started to sing. The rest of the congregation soon had the church ringing. During this hymn and another, latecomers entered and took their places.

Mr. Glasgow read the scripture for the day from the teacher's book of the Sunday School literature, then asked, "Litt, would you please lead us in prayer before we have our Sunday School classes?"

Litt Cash began to rise from his seat on the first pew. The gray hair at the top of his head glistened in the sunlight as he slowly unbent, long lean joint by long lean joint. His posture was erect and his eyes alert. However, his shirt hung loosely from his high thin shoulders. The sleeves sagged on the long slender arms that dangled to his knees. His hands poked out from the cuffs at his wrist revealing their long bony fingers. His trousers hung loosely from the tight belt at his waist. Slowly and deliberately he stepped up to the platform and knelt on one knee, bowing his head.

I can't remember exactly what he said, but it was one of the most impressive prayers I had ever heard. In our church at home we would stand and bow our heads or sit and bow our heads. I had never seen someone kneel to lead a prayer before. His language, too, was eloquent. He thanked the Lord for the recent good rain, the promise of a good harvest, the health and well-being of all the families represented in the church that day, and the safe travel of the visitors in the community. Being one of them, I was pleased. Then he began to ask the Lord to help the needy. Here he mentioned several people who were not in attendance because of sickness; he mentioned some who were not of that congregation. He brought out the need for help for several families: one whose mule had died, another where the woman of the house was too ill to cook for the family, another where fire had damaged the home. I assumed that the men who had lingered outside before Sunday School was to begin had talked about each situation, and Mr. Cash's prayer would not only reach the Lord, but those in the congregation who could do something to help. He also asked God's blessing on all those present and for the good of the world, before we joined in the Amen.

At this point we were told to go to our classes.

Four or five little ones, three to six years old, went to

the bench under the south window. Those from seven to eleven were already on the bench on the north. The young and unmarried adults came up to the choir. The married women and men stayed in their respective seats in the main section.

One of the children came and invited me to join them on the north bench, and the teacher smiled and motioned for me to come. I felt better sitting between Myrtle Mae and Lucille, so I stayed with them and listened to their class.

First the teacher read the title of the lesson and the scripture for the day. Then he asked various members of the class to read a paragraph or two of the lesson. I was interested in the tone of voice and the difference in inflection of each reader. They all softened their vowels and elided some of the consonants in what we from the North called "Southern" style. But there were differences among them. Some read rapidly and clearly, others mumbled and hesitated over some words, but all of them read and everyone was attentive. The discussion of the meaning of the lesson was interesting because there were several conflicting points of view, some of them supported and some contested by the teacher, who gave illustrations from local events or from the teacher's book he held in his hands.

We had just about finished, when the Sunday School superintendent came to the front and announced, "It's time to close. Y'all go back to your seats." When everyone had settled down, Mr. Glasgow called for another hymn, gave a closing prayer and the benediction.

While the people left the church, there was a lot of bustling and stirring about. Someone scurried around to collect the Sunday School books and tuck them onto the shelves in the lectern. Someone went out the back to be sure the lid was on the cistern. Others paused to chat as they left their seats, or stopped at the door to call a lingering child. The men clustered again at the foot of the stairs, while the young adults called back and forth among themselves.

That is when I learned the reason for all the doin's at the house this morning. Some of the girls were coming home with Myrtle Mae for Sunday dinner. Off came the shoes, and the laughing, giggling bunch trekked up the road and down the lane to Uncle Billy's house.

When we got there, two of the girls sat down in the swing and one sat in a cane-bottomed chair on the porch. Myrtle Mae, Lucille, and Dora Lamb went straight back to the kitchen. Flour sack aprons were donned over Sunday frocks and the girls pitched in. A good fire was going in the kitchen stove. Myrtle Mae got out the cast-iron skillet and put it on the stove with a big spoonful of lard. Then she put some flour in a big platter, seasoned it with salt and pepper, got the chicken, and began rolling the pieces in the flour mixture. By the time the lard was sizzling she had several pieces ready to put into the skillet. Lucille cut up the potatoes and put them into a pot to boil. Dora sliced cucumbers and tomatoes. Aunt Nancy had already rolled out the biscuits. Mary Morris set the table.

In the front room someone found a hymn book and began to play the reed organ. We could hear the soft sweet tones. Some of the girls went in with Mother and Aunt Nancy to listen and sing.

It seemed like a short while later that Myrtle Mae called the older folk and the men to come for dinner. She and Dora served the table while the rest of the girls went out to the swing and the porch. I ate with the grown-ups and the men, but I could hear the noisy chatter of the girls out front.

When we had finished and left the table the girls came

in. My what talking and laughing! They all tried to talk at once. Often there would be a little silence and then a burst of whooping and giggling. I don't know who was telling what tales but they were having a wonderful time.

Mother and Aunt Nancy went in and offered to do the dishes while the young folk visited outside. It was none too soon because a couple of boys were coming down the lane. In a short time a couple more came through the shortcut back of the orchard and another one from the field behind the barn. They seemed to have come to see William, but they knew the girls would be there. From the kitchen we could hear the blend of deep and light voices as they talked and laughed.

After while the boys headed off to the melon patch. The girls drifted by two's to the outhouse behind the chicken yard.

William led the boys back. Each of them carried either a watermelon or a couple of cantaloupes or muskmelons and laid them on the trestle table just outside the fence. Isabel took sturdy knives out to William and Uncle Billy, who cut the melons and invited everyone to come get a piece. We all took some and found chairs or benches or the swing to sit on. The conversation slowed down and became more general as the older and younger generations shared the treat and the conversation. Enough melons had been cut for second, even third helpings, for those who could eat that much. In a little while the boys got up to go home. The girls found it was time to go too.

Dora walked home with her brothers. Someone else walked with the other girls. Glenwood had come with his father's car and took Lucille. No one walked home alone.

It wasn't quite time to go get the cows and it was too hot to stay in the house, so Myrtle Mae took out her accordion with ten treble keys and two bass levers. She played and sang with enthusiasm while Aunt Nancy and Mother and I sang along on "My Old Kentucky Home," "The Wreck of the Old 97," "The Ship That Never Returned," as well as "Polly Wolly Doodle," "Barbara Allen," and so on.

It seemed terribly quiet when the young folk went home, but our singing filled the void and extended the afternoon until time for the evening chores.

CHAPTER X

Washday and New Straw in the Mattress

"Hey there! You can't stay abed today. Brush those sleepers out of your eyes and get up. We've got a lot to do."

I opened my eyes. It was almost as dark out the window now as it was when I went to bed last night. I tried to close my eyes and go to sleep again but Myrtle Mae kept talking to me.

As I tumbled off the high straw mattress, Myrtle Mae tugged at the top sheet. I got out of my pajamas and began pulling on my homemade one-piece under-drawers with a drop seat. She pulled off the bottom sheet and the quilts that lay over the mattress to keep it flat. (Straw would get compacted under the area where one slept. The mattress had to be fluffed up and smoothed out often in the summer. The quilts helped spread the weight and slow up the process.

In the winter it was good to burrow down into the straw to keep warm.) By the time I had slipped into my bib overalls and blouse, she was tugging at the mattress itself. She called for William to come upstairs to help. The big puffy straw mattress was not as heavy as it was bulky and hard to handle. It was stiffer than a feather pillow, but it did droop over her arms and puff out at the top and bottom when she tried to hold it in the middle. He grabbed it on one side while she held the other and squeezed it through the doorway and into his room at the top of the stairs.

The stairway was very narrow. The risers were steep and the treads made a turn before reaching a door that opened to several more steps down to the front bedroom. I watched them drag the mattress to the top of the stairs. Then with Myrtle Mae at the head and William at the foot of the mattress they pushed, squeezed and tugged, and grunted and sweated until it went past the door and out at the bottom of the stairs, leaving wisps and gobs of straw behind them. William carted the mattress out the front door and around the house to the orchard where Uncle Billy was trying to keep a wash from developing into a gully. He dumped the old straw onto the place and returned with the empty tick. It was made of Conestoga Ticking, a heavy durable cotton with narrow blue and white stripes. The material was made especially for straw mattresses and came sixty inches wide so it could be sewn to create any size mattress with few seams. The tick was broad around the back and overlapped almost all the way across the front to make a secure closure that would permit easy access if straw needed to be added.

I went on down to the kitchen where Mom was fixing eggs and biscuits for Jim, Billy, Grandma, and me. Uncle Billy's whole family had been up since daybreak. Separate piles of sheets and pillowcases, shirts, cotton dresses, work shirts, socks, and I don't know what else, were in the front room.

Mother stated, "When you have finished your breakfast, we will go down to the pond behind the stable. Nancy and Myrtle Mae will do the wash today and I will help them. Some of our things need washing too. Your grandmother will stay here in the house. It's too hot and there's no good place for her to sit down there. She will probably read her Bible. Kak and Billy, you can stay here with her if you promise not to bother her, or you can come down there if you will keep out of the way. Jim and William will be helping."

William and Jim piled some of the clothes on Uncle Billy's homemade wheelbarrow and took them down to Aunt Nancy. Later they came for the rest of them. When Mother and Grandmother had finished with the dishes, we too went down.

The pond was large with an easy slope to the water at the front, but at the back near the woods the dirt was mounded up and created sort of a levee. It rose a few feet above the water and was wide enough for two abreast to walk on it. All the laundry things were there. At the north end a large open cast iron kettle full of white sheets and boiling water sat on legs over a small bed of coals. Nearby was a long wooden bench with three zinc wash tubs on it.

When we got there, Aunt Nancy was using a stick with a smooth rounded end to take the sheets that had just been boiled out of the kettle and put them in the middle tub of rinse water. They had been hand washed with lye soap on the washboard in the largest zinc wash tub before being put into the iron kettle to boil. Aunt Nancy still made her own lye soap with pork fat and ashes and lye. (I don't know the process but every household that could made its own soap. Mother and Aunt Nancy agreed that it cleaned better and was easier on the hands than any of the commercial soaps they could buy.)

Now Myrtle Mae rinsed the sheets, wrung them out by hand, and then put them in the bluing water. She wrung them out again, careful to keep the water falling back into the bluing tub before hanging them up. William had strung some wire between the corner of the stable and a tall sturdy pole fastened to a fence post to hang them on. There was a long light pole to prop up the wire after the clothes were hung to keep them from dragging on the ground.

While Aunt Nancy helped rinse and hang out the sheets and other white clothes, Mother was washing some of the colored things and socks that didn't need to be boiled. She needed more hot wash water, so she dipped several saucepans of it out of the kettle and poured it into the wash tub.

She called for William, who got another bucket of water from the pond to fill the kettle. He was the only one tall enough and strong enough to lean over the bank and fill the bucket from the deepest part of the pond without disturbing the mud at the bottom. The water soon came to a boil again.

The two huge bed ticks in the wash tub became heavy and awkward to handle in the hot water, but Aunt Nancy and Myrtle Mae worked together on them until they were ready to be put into the boiling water.

Finally it was time for the overalls. They were dirty with dust and grease and tobacco stains. Old faded ones were soft and easy to wash; the newer ones were hard to rub on the washboard. Regardless, they were scrubbed and put into the boiling water too.

Uncle Billy and William liked to work in the soft faded overalls. New overalls were made of heavy, dark blue denim with white stitching.

"They look good but they're as stiff as boards. They

practically crackle when I sit down or bend over. They don't feel at all good 'til they've been washed a dozen times," William complained.

When William wasn't needed he still had to stay within calling distance, so he spent his time in the tack room mending harness or sharpening tools. Jim stayed with William most of the time, but he was the one who took down and put up the clothes pole when dried clothes were exchanged for wet ones. Bill and I stayed around in the lot, startling frogs and watching them jump into the water along the bank at the shallow side of the pond. Some of the time we watched William work.

We saw a tall straw stack just outside of the temporary fence on the south side of the lot. A pole sticking out at the top of this gleaming golden stack seemed to call us to climb the pile and reach it. We were eyeing our chances when Mother saw us looking at it. Mind reader that she was, she called to us.

"Billy. Kak. Don't try to climb the straw stack. Your Uncle Billy had that stack made when his wheat was threshed last week. The straw on top is laid so water will drain off the stack instead of seeping down into the rest of it. If you climb it you will ruin it."

On this sunny, breezy day the light and white things usually dried by the time the next tub of clothes was ready. Around ten o'clock everything had been dried and taken in except the bed ticks and the overalls. William and Jim went to find Uncle Billy. The rest of us went back to the house. The baskets of clothes were put in the back hall as we all went to the back porch to draw water from the cistern.

Mom, Myrtle Mae, and Aunt Nancy each took some soap, washcloth and towel and a pan of water to their rooms to clean up and change into fresh clothes.

As she went into the room where our suitcases were,

Mother said, "I never can use the washboard without getting sloshed all over in front."

Myrtle Mae paused and replied, "I get wet on my shoulder and back too. I have to throw one end of the sheets over my shoulder to keep them off the ground until I get them wrung out," and went on upstairs.

"Not only that but I perspired so. I'm glad we could kick our muddy shoes off on the back steps. We can clean them off after they've dried," Aunt Nancy added.

Billy and I stayed on the back porch and washed our faces and hands.

Uncle Billy, William, and Jim came in a few minutes before dinner was ready, washed their faces and hands and sat on the front porch waiting to be called. They said that they had shoveled and leveled a load of sand over the straw that William had strewn in the wash at the back of the orchard. Uncle Billy planned to spread a few bales of hay over the spot to hold the dirt and allow some of the seeds in the hay to sprout so the roots would hold the soil.

Billy and I told him how much we admired that big stack of straw and speculated on how difficult it would be to climb. With an amused gleam in his eye Uncle Billy said, "Well now, I expect we'll be using some of that straw this afternoon. Mebby you can test yourselves. I'll have to top it again anyway."

Elated, Billy and I went to the kitchen eager for dinner. After dinner Uncle Billy sat quietly on a chair in the shade of the oak trees by the front fence for a little while, then went down toward the stable. I don't know where Jim and William went. Billy and I were sent up the lane to the mailbox while dishes were being done.

When the dishtowels were hung on the line beside the back steps, we traipsed down to the stable again. Mother took down the overalls and carried the clothesbasket back to the house. Billy and I stayed at the stable hoping to climb the straw stack.

Uncle Billy was there and laughingly said, "All right now, let's see you get up to the top." The slippery stuff wasn't as easy to climb as it looked. The straw was slick and if you didn't get each foot planted inside the stack, as you climbed you could slip back or fall. When Jim saw us slipping and trying to get a secure footing, he joined us. We all reached the top and didn't do much damage to the straw stack either.

That little challenge being over, Billy and I went back to the house with Mom. Soon we saw Myrtle Mae and Aunt Nancy coming to the house with an enormous blue and white striped ball. When they got closer we could see that it was the mattress ticking stuffed overly full and in an unrecognizable mass. I wondered, "How will anyone sleep on that?"

I held the door for them, and they put the thing on the slats of Aunt Nancy's bed. Then they began pushing straw into the corners and along the sides. Gradually it took shape. They punched down the middle, almost like kneading bread. Finally they folded the overlapping part down and smoothed it all out. They took a big heavy quilt that lay on the trunk under the window and spread it over the straw mattress. Aunt Nancy went about putting clean sheets on the bed and a clean cover on the bolster that went all across the bed like a long pillow.

Myrtle Mae had gone back to the stable where William was stuffing her mattress. In a little while they came to the house with a similar bundle and with a lot of huffing and puffing pushed and pulled it up to Myrtle's room. William must have helped her spread the straw, for they both came down the stairs later with an air of finality and relief.

William and Uncle Billy had dumped the wash water

and put the kettle and the tubs away. The bench was placed at the side of the breezeway in the stable.

Aunt Nancy's reclining rocker was near the trunk by the window of her room. She set the back of the rocker into the reclining position and sat down. She picked up the mail that Billy and I had brought from the mailbox and said, "Thank you for getting the mail. It has been a hard day and I think I may get a headache if I don't rest awhile."

Mother, having rested while Aunt Nancy and Myrtle Mae wrestled with the straw mattress, came into the room and suggested that Billy and I should accompany her to the back of the garden to pick grapes. Myrtle Mae must have rested too because I didn't see her again until late in the afternoon when it was time to get the cows.

Behind the stable lot there was a woods and behind it was a pasture field. Uncle Billy had put the cows there because it was close to the house and there were no good hiding places in it. He knew Myrtle Mae might be too tired to go traipsing over Grandmother's farm looking for them today. It really was a comparatively short walk and the cattle were easy to find except that one cow had gotten down into a gully with pools of water in the bottom and some good grass along the banks. Myrtle Mae knew the hiding places in that field so well that she just went over to the bank and yelled at the cow. Soon it came up a slope that led to the field and joined the rest of the cows headed back to the barn.

On the way through the woods I asked Myrtle Mae about the kinds of trees that we were passing. She named them as I pointed to them. We also saw old nut hulls, some whole and some broken open, by squirrels I suppose. One thing looked like a smooth round nut that I had never seen. I picked it up. It was lighter than a nut and had a tiny hole in it. I asked, "What's this?"

Myrtle looked at it and said, "It's an oak gall."

"What's an oak gall?"

"It's made by some kind of an insect that infests the oak trees. You see them all around. If you break one open a lot of fine brown powder comes out. Pappy says that in the old times and during the Civil War people mixed that powder with water and something else to use for ink. See, they're all over the place. They don't seem to kill the trees."

About that time I heard the bleating of Uncle Billy's sheep on the other side of the woods.

"Oh, oh, we'd better hurry. Get on, you cows!"

"Why the rush?" I asked.

"Pappy told William to turn the sheep into the pasture we just left when we got into the stable lot. I guess he didn't check the lot, and he let them into this field early. He didn't figure I'd have a stubborn cow. Get along there! The female sheep are no problem, but Billy Buck, the ram, is mean. He butts anyone or anything he sees. Pappy and William can handle him but I just have to get out of the way. Shake a leg, Kak. He could hurt you."

Myrtle had the cows hurrying, herself trotting, and me running to keep up. We got through the gate, and Myrtle Mae had just shut it, when Billy Buck came charging toward us and banged his head against the gate. The whole thing shook, but stood firm.

"Billy Buck hits the gates so often Pappy has to put up a new one every year or so."

When the milking was done and supper over, everyone was tired enough to go to bed, but the sun had shown brightly all day and it was too hot to be comfortable in the house. We all sat outside, either on the porch or the swing between the oak trees, or on the bench by the front fence. Myrtle Mae played her concertina and Mother and Aunt Nancy and I sang. Sometimes William and Jim and Bill joined in. Uncle Billy just listened or talked to the boys. We all slapped at mosquitoes. Those who slept downstairs went in fairly early. Myrtle Mae and I stayed out a lot longer.

It was a pretty moonlit night. We talked about the sky and looked for the stars. The sky was too bright to see them well, but we found what constellations we could. We talked about the crickets, jar flies, cicadas, and locusts that were giving a concert until she thought it was time to go in.

We had talked quietly and no one called out to us. We made our way through the front bedroom, where Uncle Billy and Aunt Nancy were sleeping, and up the stairs. I could feel it getting hotter with every rising step. Even after the sun went down and the dew had fallen, it was hot! Uncle Billy had built his house himself and had put a tin roof on it just as he had on the barn. There was no wooden sheathing, just long sheets of galvanized metal nailed to strips of wood. The sun on the tin roof acted like the fire under an oven. It was baking hot! No wonder Uncle Billy didn't complain at our staying outside so long.

There was no one in William's room. Myrtle Mae mumbled, "I saw the boys going down to the stable with a flashlight. They will probably gig frogs for a while. William does it sometimes to keep busy until the room gets cool enough for him to sleep."

We went on into our room, got into our night things in a hurry and then climbed onto the straw mattress. Even with all the poking and kneading that had been done the straw compressed under our weight and we each had a little depression to sleep in.

Although the room was stifling hot, there was a fresh odor of clean straw. Tired from the long washday we soon went to sleep.

CHAPTER XI

A Pig's Tail and Uncle Eddy's Tale

We always spent several days with Aunt Linnie and Uncle Herman. Aunt Linnie was really Mother's cousin, but they were such close playmates and companions when they were children, they felt like sisters. It was easier for Bill and Jim and me to call her Aunt than Cousin. Most of the five children in their family stair-stepped us. Glenwood was a little older than Jim. Elbert was a little older than I, and Earl was a little older than Billy. We usually followed them and tried to "help" with the numerous chores. I didn't follow Lucille, their sister, much. Although she was just a little older than Glenwood, she and Aunt Linnie's sister, Mamie, who was about the same age as Lucille, mostly worked around the house with the cooking, cleaning, and sewing. It wasn't as interesting to me as the outside work. However, I enjoyed going to the garden or the hen house with them. They treated me as an equal, letting me pick beans, shell peas, and gather eggs with them. They talked with me, answered my questions, and patiently put up with my incessant chatter.

I wondered why they always shooed the hens off the nests before gathering the eggs in the hen house. That was, until the day a chicken snake rose up and slid out of the nest as the hen squawked, and fluttered off. The snake slithered away; Mamie and I were backing out the door but Lucille grabbed a hoe that was kept handy in a corner, and cut off its head.

Glenwood was usually out of the house working with Uncle Herman, but even when he was at the house, he was a little aloof and sat around quietly watching us with an amused expression. Jim was left on his own to find things to do.

Milking time at Aunt Linnie's was, again, one of my favorite parts of the day. Then, almost everyone was together in the barn lot. Elbert and Earl (and possibly Jim) would have gone into the field and driven the cows up to the barn where Aunt Linnie, Lucille, and Mamie would be waiting. There were usually ten to fourteen cows to milk and it took a long time. While they were milking, Glenwood, Elbert, and Earl would be "slopping the hogs" and feeding the pigs. The hogs were in a lot next to the barn lot and shared the pond with the cows. There was a long trough into which corn and waste from the preparation of meals and the table scraps including the dishwater were poured. We weren't allowed to go into the hog lot at feeding time. Even Aunt Linnie's boys made sure they didn't get between the hogs and their food. They were greedy and fought, grunted, snorted, and squealed as they clambered up to the troughs. Anyone caught between them and the slop could be knocked over and trampled, even bitten, in the crazed competition.

Feeding the pigs was a different matter. The baby pigs were only a few weeks old and were fed in a shed apart from the hogs. Their little rounded pink bodies would nudge and squirm until they were shoulder to shoulder at their feeding trough. Elbert or Earl encouraged Bill and me to catch and hold the back legs of the piglets while they were eating. We grasped their legs all right, but I had never felt such kicking or heard such squealing! It was impossible to hold on. For such little creatures, they were powerfully strong and agile.

On the sly we were told about the time Elbert got a new bone-handled pocketknife with a sharp shiny blade. He was proud of it and wanted to see just how sharp it was. To test it he caught one of the little pigs and sliced at its tail with his knife. He was surprised to see that he had really cut off the pig's tail. The little thing went squealing all over the lot with blood trailing from its bare behind. He and Earl worried lest their father find out what he had done, herded the noisy piglet to the other side of the shed away from the house. It looked like the pig was going to bleed forever. They waited until the pig had quieted down with the other pigs before they came in for supper. Everyone else had almost finished eating when they got in. Uncle Herman grumbled a bit about their being late but he never noticed the pig without a tail, and no one "squealed" on Elbert. His worry was punishment enough.

He didn't end his experiments with the pig. Elbert had two toes that were grown together when he was born. They didn't interfere with his walking or give him any trouble, but he wanted them separated and figured that he could do it himself with his fine sharp knife. He soon found out that cutting hurt, and the toe bled almost as much as the pig. Aunt Linnie came upon him sitting on the porch step with his foot in a wash pan of water trying to stop the bleeding. In her kind way she bandaged his toe and soothed his pain, as one would for a boy too big to cry and too young to bandage his own foot. In the years we were visiting them he had quit worrying about his toe. In all the summers we spent with them, going barefoot most of the time, I don't remember ever noticing his double toe. I don't know which toe or which foot was affected.

Uncle Herman sold cream to the local dairy, so after the milking was done, Aunt Linnie, Lucille, and Mamie would take the buckets to the separator to skim off the cream. The separator consisted of a big metal bowl into which the milk was poured. At the bottom there was a pipe that led to a series of filter disks. When the handle was turned the milk would spin through the series of disks. The cream was forced through a spout at the top where it would be caught and strained into a galvanized milk can. It was closed with a tight top and put in front of the house for pick up in the morning. The milk was filtered through a spout at the bottom and poured out into a can to be used at home. Whatever milk the family didn't use was fed to the hogs and pigs.

The separator parts had to be washed clean and boiling water poured over them when the work was finished. Often it was dark before we all got back into the house. Then it was supper by lamplight before we went to bed.

At Uncle Herman's house I didn't ever know for sure where everyone slept. Billy and I were put to bed early. There was a day bed or cot in what I thought was Lucille and Mamie's room. Bill was placed at the head and me at the foot. We were short enough at that time that our feet didn't touch and we were usually so tired we went right to sleep.

By the time we got up, morning chores, including the milking, were done and breakfast dishes were being placed around the table.

The house was built like an L with two rooms separated

by a hall across the front and two more rooms behind the west front room. A wide screened porch ran along the back of the front room then down the side to the end of the house. The dining table was kept on the porch in the summer.

On sunny hot days we sat there snapping beans, peeling potatoes, shelling peas and preparing the garden vegetables for dinner. Just as it was at Uncle Billy's, when there was a lull in the day's work, it seemed that there were apples to peel. It was easier and cooler to dry apples in the summer. Cooking them and making dried-apple butter was better done in the winter. Nothing tastes better than a hot biscuit with a glob of rich dried-apple butter on it. It was then that Mom and Aunt Linnie exchanged news about their various childhood friends and family and recalled various humorous incidents of their growing-up years. Lucille and Mamie often commented on some of the stories that differed from what they had heard, and Mother or Aunt Linnie reasoned out the discrepancies. I snapped beans and listened.

When Aunt Linnie thought enough apples were peeled and cut, she handed Lucille an old sheet and asked her to put it on the tin roof of the porch on the west side of the house. After Lucille got the old wooden ladder, climbed up onto the roof and got things ready, Mamie handed her the buckets of apples to spread out. In a couple of days they were dry and ready to be brought down to Aunt Linnie, who poured them into clean flour sacks for storage until winter. I wondered which was the hardest task, Myrtle Mae's working her large long frame through the small, low window onto Uncle Billy's front porch roof to spread the apples, or Lucille's climbing the old wooden ladder to the porch roof at her house to do the same thing.

I enjoyed some of the hot days, when Uncle Eddie, Mother's brother, sat leaning back against a pile of sacks of dried apples stacked on the floor of the porch, and told us about his young days. He worked on the rivers, sometimes the Ohio, sometimes the Red River near Clarksville, Tennessee, and then on the ferries in Kuttawa or Eddyville. He also told us about his work with the farmers in the area. They usually hired him to run the steam engines that ran the threshing machines. He had some exciting stories about how one engine blew up or another that almost blew up and frightened the men bringing in the wheat. His stories fascinated me because he would be dramatic or winsome or spooky, depending on the story.

He was also the one who told me that my grandfather was stolen by Gypsies when he was young. They forced him to work on the riverboats between Cairo, Illinois, and New Orleans. I hardly believed him, since Mother had told me that her father ran away from home when he was young. However, I have learned that the people of southern Illinois who lived near Cairo, Thebes, or Karnak were called Gypsies and his home was in Golconda, Illinois, on the Ohio River and near these other cities. It could have been as Uncle Eddie said.

It was good to work sheltered on the cool porch in a light rain. On those days the boys and Uncle Herman would leave their work in the barn or the tack house or the garage and come sit with us and visit. They would have other types of stories and jokes on one another to keep things lively.

On the days when there were heavy rains or thunderstorms, we would move into the house because a driving rain from the right direction would soak the whole porch.

CHAPTER XII

Guineas in the Chicken House?

One hot afternoon when we were all out on Aunt Linnie's back porch peeling peaches, Mother noticed a dark cloud coming up in the northeast. About that time the tassels of the corn in the field beside the house began to rustle and bend, and it became a little chilly on the porch. Aunt Linnie laid down her knife and her pan of peelings saying, "We'd better get the chickens into the hen house. It looks as if it will be a hard rain." The chickens were not in a fenced chicken yard. They foraged all around the farmhouse and outbuildings. Calling "Chick, chick, chick," Mother and we children went to the front to turn them toward the back of the house. Lucille and Mamie went out to the garden and the cornfield. Aunt Linnie opened the chicken house and scattered a little grain in front to encourage them to hurry and then herded them in and closed the door. That done, everyone headed back to the porch.

Billy and I happened to see a couple of the wild guinea hens and chicks that had been near the house mingling with the other chickens and became concerned about them. We asked Aunt Linnie if they shouldn't be put in the chicken house because they would get cold and wet too. Mom said they would probably be all right outside. Aunt Linnie said she didn't think they'd come to the chicken house. Lucille and Mamie said they usually went to their nests in the cornfield. Billy and I persisted in our concern, so, finally, Aunt Linnie said, "If you can get them up to the door of the chicken house, we'll let them go in."

With that Billy and I started on our errand of mercy. The guineas had moved into the cornfield while the chickens were gathered into the house. Billy went onto the field from the right side. I went in from the left. We hoped to get behind them and run them back into the yard. At first we moved slowly to keep from exciting them. They just meandered off, slowly going deeper and deeper into the field. Then, as the wind rose, we tried to hurry. They just hurried faster, darting first one way and then another, always succeeding in getting behind us or barely out of reach or suddenly seeming to disappear altogether. We decided we would not be able to herd them back to the house but would have to catch them. We ran after them and sometimes came within an inch of grasping one when she would fly almost in our faces and land several rows away. The saber-edged corn leaves caught at our clothes, scratched our bare arms and legs, and helped conceal the guineas. When the first drops of rain began to fall on us, we were glad to give up our chase and run, tired and out of breath, back to the porch. We decided that if the guineas didn't want help they could just get wet. We didn't know that the guineas were really wild and lived like quails and whip-poor-wills in the open. They were encouraged to stay with the tame chickens because they were as good as dogs at creating a noise and rousing the house at night if anything unusual like a fox or a stranger came about the house.

The rain had beaten down heavily for a long while when Uncle Herman came in with the boys. He said, "It has been so dry all spring and summer that the cistern is very low. I think we had better catch some of this water. It has rained hard enough and long enough to wash off the roof. Earl, set up the trough."

I had expected Earl to have to go out into the rain and put the trough under the downspout of the gutter. I didn't see how he would direct the water into the cistern on the porch. However, he took the top off the cistern and placed the mouth of the trough on it. Then he moved a little slab of wood and uncovered an opening in the clapboard siding. He slid the other end of the wooden trough out of the opening to meet the downspout from the roof. Last he ran some bailing wire from a nail on the wall under the trough and back to the nail again to hold the trough in position. The water poured into the cistern with the force and sound of a big waterfall. All conversation was cut off by the welcome sound of the water.

Farm families usually filled their cisterns in the winter when the rainwater was cold. Water was apt to turn sour if the temperature in the cistern got above 50 degrees. Uncle Herman decided to chance the poor water, because this had been a dry year and the water in the cistern was very low.

In a little while Aunt Linnie and Mom and Lucille and Mamie rose and went into the kitchen. There they busied themselves clearing stale food out of the "safe," and putting more flour and corn meal into bins under the kitchen cabinet. Someone would be going to town the next day, so they separated the eggs that would be traded for groceries from those that would be used at home. Then they found a little mending to do and their visiting went on while their hands were busy.

Glenwood and his dad rocked back on their cane-bottomed chairs and discussed the crop, the horse and mules, the fences, and tomorrow's tasks while Earl scrunched down on a couple of bags of dried apples and took a nap. Elbert went to another corner of the porch near where his grandfather, who was also my Uncle Eddy, sat chewing tobacco and drowsing. Uncle Eddy noticed Elbert pull a little piece of wood and his new knife out of his pocket. "Better watch you don't cut yerself," he mumbled.

Jim was a Boy Scout at home and was interested in Elbert's use of the knife. Billy and I came over to watch, sitting cross-legged on the floor. Seeing that he had an audience close by, Uncle Eddy roused up and began to tell us about his living at iron hill and his work at one of the iron furnaces. He told us about a local man named Kelly, who invented a new method of making steel. Some of the employees at Kelly's furnace learned the process and moved to England where they set up a factory and took credit for inventing what is now known as Bessemer Steel. Kelly died bankrupt, and his heirs sued the English company for stealing the process. The case was still in court. Uncle Eddy also mentioned other ironworks over between the rivers. He was a good storyteller with a great gift for details, a penchant for exaggeration and humorous understatement. His rich sense of humor and appreciation of the ridiculous filled his stories with chuckles and laughter. His embellishments caused him to be accused of making his stories up. However, he once stated that a good story was like a piece of elastic. The more sure the base of the story, the further it could be stretched before it broke (became unbelievable).

Billy and I were just getting absorbed in another of Uncle

Eddy's tales when Uncle Herman announced, "The rain has tapered off. You boys had better get the cows. It's getting late."

Earl roused from his nap and began to roll up his pant legs, "Its goin' tuh be muddy out there."

Elbert pocketed his knife and started gathering the chips from his whittling. Lucille approached with a broom and dustpan, "You go ahead. I'll clean up your mess. It's late. It'll soon be sundown and we don't want to milk in the dark if we can help it."

Bill, Jim, and I stayed in the house. Mom didn't want us to get our shoes all muddy and our feet weren't hardened enough to go barefoot.

While the boys were gone, Aunt Linnie, Lucille, and Mamie got up the leftovers from the meals of the day, including the scraps of vegetables and peelings from their preparation, and scraped them into the big pail where the dishwater had been poured. Soon the cowbell could be heard nearing the barn lot. All three of them put on rubber boots and went out the back door to do the evening chores. Lucille and Mamie carried the "slop bucket" between them, careful not to slosh the contents on themselves.

Since Uncle Herman and Glenwood had gone to the stable, we were alone in the house. Mother and Uncle Eddy began to talk about old family things. Mother was about twenty years younger than he was, so he told her a lot about his growing up and working with his father on various ferryboats down in Tennessee. We three children sat and listened.

In a little while we could hear everyone return from milking the cows and feeding the pigs. Aunt Linnie stepped into the back porch, took off her boots, and crossed the kitchen to the side porch. She filled a wash pan and took it to the back porch for the boys to clean off their feet and legs before they came in. Lucille and Mamie had already taken off their boots. One of them set about lighting a couple of lamps. By the time they had finished the milking and washed the separator, dark had set in. Aunt Linnie got the leftovers from the noon dinner and put them on the table on the side porch. In addition to the corn, beans, and squash, there was a lot of corn bread, some biscuits, and milk. My favorite evening eating was sorghum molasses mixed with a big dab of homemade butter, spread good and thick on a hunk of cornbread, and followed with a big gulp of sweet milk. Elbert and Earl liked the buttermilk better but I was happy with my choices.

The only problem with that meal was the cleanup afterward. I always succeeded in getting the sticky combination of sorghum and butter not only on my fingers but also on my hands, wrists, lower arms, elbows, and my overalls. Mother always checked me after I washed to be sure I didn't miss any sticky spots that might rub off on the sheets. She had to do the same for Billy before she picked up one of the lamps and took us to bed. Later she checked our overalls and sponged them off to be ready for the next day.

CHAPTER XIII

Lucille Conquers the Muddy Road

The next morning I woke to the sounds of Mother, Aunt Linnie, and Uncle Herman's voices. Although they were talking quietly, I could hear tension in Mother's voice. The gist of the matter was that Uncle Herman couldn't drive to town and take Mother and me with him as they had planned. The wind and rain yesterday had damaged the corn crop in the fertile bottomlands that he had rented along the Cumberland River. Almost all of his corn was planted there. He had to ride his horse Fred over the muddy fields to see what he could do about it. Lucille would have to do his errands and drive the car. Mother was afraid to ride in the car with Lucille driving it.

Normally Mother was courageous. I had never seen her cringe in any family crisis. She could mend our wounds, even some serious ones. She seemed to be the doctor's aide during family illnesses. She confronted our schoolteachers and principals when necessary. She spoke at P.T.A. and other meetings, and generally handled emergencies calmly and effectively. However, Mother was afraid of riding in cars. She was always concerned about who would do the driving. She was not truly comfortable even when Dad was at the wheel. Country roads bothered her, and wet country roads worried her obsessively.

Lucille was about sixteen years old. Mother thought of her as one of the children, but Uncle Herman and Aunt Linnie explained that Lucille had been driving over that same road to the high school in town for a long time. In fact she only drove on rainy days, otherwise she would ride Fred. Mother reluctantly accepted the fact that Lucille would drive.

When we were ready to go, we walked down a little slope to the garage near the edge of the road. Apprehensively, Mother helped me into the front seat of the car and then started to get into it herself. The car was on a rise and the running board was high off the ground. Mother's legs were short and her skirt was narrow. Looking around to see if anyone else was near, she heisted her skirt above her knee and got her foot on the running board. She grasped the car door and the back of the seat, pulled herself up, and swung onto the seat of the car.

"I may as well have tried to get my foot into the stirrups of a saddle," she huffed. "Well, almost. I really couldn't have gotten on a horse."

Lucille went around to the driver's side and reached up to the two levers on an arc of metal, much like the arc of a protractor, attached to the steering rod just behind the wheel. She set them at a particular angle and then went to the front of the car. With both hands she grabbed the crank that stuck out below the radiator and pulled it around twice.

Nothing happened. She came back to the steering wheel and re-adjusted the little rods. Then she cranked the car again. This time there was a cough and a sputter. She got into the car and sat down behind the wheel, kicked each of the three pedals on the floorboard, re-set the emergency brake and one of the levers on the steering wheel, and climbed out again. "This time it better go!" she said in a determined voice and vigorously turned the crank again. Obediently it sputtered, coughed, and then began to chug smoothly. She swung up to the driver's seat, released the emergency brake, put the gear in reverse, and backed out of the garage.

She backed a little way up the rise that led to the house and then started forward to the road. That area was fairly level and had a good gravelly base. We started off well. Mother's eyes darted back and forth and she bit her lower lip. I could see that she was apprehensive.

Lucille sat calmly. Her hold on the steering wheel seemed relaxed but she was watching the road intently. On this level stretch the Ford jiggled a little as it followed the ruts formed by the last wagon that had gone by. Lucille was still breathing a little heavily from her exertions with the crank. I remembered that Dad felt that getting the car started was the hardest part of driving. It took a lot of muscle to turn the crank, and your arm could be broken if the crank jerked back while you still had hold of it.

Suddenly the car overrode the ruts and began to angle sideways. Mother took a deep gasp of breath and held it as the car oozed over to the edge of the road. The rear wheels began to slide toward the little drainage ditch along there. Lucille got the front turned in the right direction, the car slowly straightened itself toward the middle of the road, and we went on. Mother released her breath in a long sigh.

Two boards that were laid from one side of the road to

the other formed a bridge across a little ditch. The boards were just enough higher than the roadbed to cause the car to bump. It could have sent us into another slide but it didn't. The force of the jolt jarred the breath out of Mom so she could neither gasp nor sigh. I bounced. There was a little rise where the gravel base rose from under the dirt and the tires found good traction, but not for long.

We entered a place where the roadbed ran between two steep banks. They were almost vertical, and if the car happened to nose into either one of them we would be firmly stuck. Just when it looked as if the front bumper would imbed itself in the bank on the right, Lucille calmly jostled the steering wheel and we skimmed by it. Her expression didn't change, but I could see her hands stiffen and relax on the wheel as we went toward one bank and then the other. Mother inhaled audibly between closely pursed lips and grabbed the door handle, holding it and her breath until the car was straight in the road.

We crossed one broad creek where there was no bridge, and Lucille drove down into it carefully watching the water to be sure it wasn't high enough to stall the car. Then on the solid gravel of the creek bed she stomped on the gas pedal to give us enough momentum to carry us up the other side.

The slipping and sliding, gasping and sighing continued for the next few miles until we reached the high hill that led downward into town.

This hill was about as steep as the first downhill on a monster roller coaster. It was bad enough to go down it in dry weather in a slow moving wagon with the brakes held tightly lest the wagon would overrun the team. It was awesome in the car. It was being impelled too fast while veering from side to side on the slushy surface of the road.

For several yards the car slid almost completely sideways

down the incline, leaning as if it were trying to tip over. Lucille got the front wheels back in line only to have to do the same maneuver on the right. Toward the lower end of the road there were gullies by the roadside that the car lurched toward and then away from as Lucille twirled the wheel this way and that. She didn't dare apply the brakes too firmly or the car would slide out of control. I watched her gently coax them to restrain our progress.

Finally, the road leveled off near the Kuttawa Mineral Springs. Gravel had been liberally poured on the road from here to the center of town, and we made an easy approach to a parking place in front of Hugh Wake's store.

Mother, obviously relieved, half stepped and half jumped down and turned to help me out of the car. Putting me down on the ground, she looked at Lucille and said, "That was quite a ride! Lucille, you can do more things with this car than a monkey can with a coconut!"

The ride home was equally slippery and exciting, but Mother's gasps and sighs were not as deep or as often. From that day on, Lucille was the only driver she would ride with when we stayed at Aunt Linnie's.

CHAPTER XIV

Who Won the Cake?
Who Got the Pickles?

One day Elbert and Earl came home from Shelby School bubbling over about the Box Supper that would be held there Saturday night. "She said to tell everyone to come."

At times when the teacher felt she needed supplies that the school board did not provide and were too numerous or too expensive to buy herself, she would devise some entertainment for the community to bring in the money. In the summer this was usually a supper of some kind, a pie supper in which the older girls would bring a pie or cake to be auctioned off, or a box supper. This was to be a Box Supper.

Since Lucille and Mamie were not "going with" any special fellow, they said I could come along with them. Anyone in the community could take part. The unmarried girls would pack a box with food for two. The boxes would be auctioned off, and the man or boy who paid the highest price for the box got to sit with the girl while they shared its contents. Lucille and Mamie took boxes. Glenwood, Jim, and Elbert took pocket money.

Most of the time the girls had a great deal of fun taking the kidding and teasing during the auction, and good-naturedly ate with whoever won their boxes.

Often Estina Riley, the teacher and self-appointed auctioneer, would speculate on the contents of the box. "I think this one must have slices of coconut cake," she might say, or "This one feels like it contains some cherry, or apple, or peach pie." This would encourage the bidding. Sometimes she'd say something outlandish such as, "This one is heavy. I bet it has pickled pigs feet and crowder peas in it."

The girl who had brought the box would yell out, "It does not. It has fried chicken, baked beans, potato salad, biscuits, and lemon chess pie." This very effectively revealed the owner of the box. Everyone would laugh and, of course, bidding would be heavy while the boys who liked her competed for her favor with their wallets.

Supposedly no one knew who had prepared the boxes, but sometimes a girl would tie it with a special ribbon or identify the box in some way so that her particular beau could recognize it.

There was one very pretty box that two fellows seemed to recognize. A tall good-looking, good-natured, muscular fellow, on the far side of the crowd bid two dollars. That was pretty steep for an opening bid. A tall lanky fellow with a ready grin, reddish hair, and new overalls standing near me bid two dollars and twenty-five cents. Someone intervened and bid two dollars and fifty cents. Bidder number one went up another quarter. The lanky boy bid three dollars.

Another outsider upped the ante by twenty-five cents,

and bidders one and two countered with further raises. That froze out the other bidders. After two more bids the lanky boy was out of money. With serious purpose he began nudging his friends and holding out his hand. They laughed and kidded him, but one or another handed him a coin. "Good looking" was a little older than "Lanky" and may have had some livestock and cropland of his own. "Lanky" and his friends were probably still working for their Dads and hiring themselves out for cash money when they could. The bidding went on while "Lanky" continued to touch his friends for support. His raises dropped to ten cents, then five. Finally "Lanky" had to resign himself to defeat. Neither he nor his friends had any money left. I could see the anguish on the boy's face. Although he didn't let them fall, there were tears in his eyes. His shoulders drooped and he breathed heavily. Soon, red-faced and solemn, he and two of his friends quietly left the crowd.

Meanwhile, the bidding for other boxes proceeded until they were all gone and the young folk were consuming their contents.

After a little while Estina rose from the bench where she was sitting, sharing her box with her current beau, and announced, "Now we have a cake," she held up a huge three-layer cake with white icing sprinkled with coconut, "to be given to the prettiest girl."

All the girls who wanted to compete lined up. The cake would be held over the head of each one and the crowd would applaud or shout. The one for whom the loudest and noisiest sound was made got the cake.

The winner was the girl for whom "Lanky" had bankrupted himself and his friends.

"Now we will give this jar of pickles to the ugliest boy. Are there any nominations?"

Names were shouted out with a flurry of hoots and

hollers! Finally, a winner was declared and someone, a big burly fellow that everyone seemed to like, grinned and wisecracked to the crowd as he strolled up to the porch to collect his dubious prize.

It had been a good and fun-filled evening and the people began to disperse. Some had come in buggies or wagons. Some had ridden horseback, but most had walked. The families and couples left, going up or down the road. Our group, Lucille and Mamie, the young men that had eaten with them, Elbert, Jim, and I went down the road and turned off at the first fork, heading back to Aunt Linnie's. Glenwood was with another group. I supposed he was seeing some girl home.

I thought of "Lanky" and felt sorry for his disappointment. The song "After the Ball" was still popular. Part of the chorus came to mind. "Many a heart is aching, If you could read them all; Many the hopes that have vanished, After the ball." I thought that hearts could ache after a box supper too.

A few years later I saw a mature "Lanky" and a more-mature "girl" coming out of Espie's Shoe Store across the street. They were walking together, each holding a hand of a red-headed little one toddling between them in a pair of new shoes. "Lanky's" heart may have ached but his hopes had not vanished.

CHAPTER XV

Fred and Kate

Uncle Herman's horse, Fred, made the visits with Aunt Linnie and Uncle Herman extra special to Billy and me.

Fred was about fifteen hands high with graceful lean lines, a proud bearing, erect head, alert ears, and eyes that looked at you kindly. When the sun struck him he gleamed a deep coppery color called chestnut or sorrel, his entire figure burnished by the light. His most distinguishing mark was the long white blaze extending from the forelock down his face to the bridge of his nose.

His muzzle was soft as velvet and his lips were tender when he took corn from our hands. His ears turned attentively when we talked to him. He liked to be scratched behind the ears and rubbed down the front of his long face. He loved it when Lucille brushed and curried him. He even appeared to stand taller and more proudly when she had finished.

He stood quietly when Elbert walked around him. Earl even walked under his stomach to his other side and he didn't stir. "He won't move if you don't bump or brush against him. Even if you do, he just lifts his hoof like he was sweepin' a fly. He wouldn't hurt you."

Fred seemed to have his own notion of his place in the horse world. Whenever he was ridden with another horse or group of horses he liked to be in front. Lucille told us that she rode him to the high school in town during the school year. "If I got out late in the afternoon and the others I rode with went on ahead, I'd have to get on him quickly or he'd take off like lightning before I could get a good hold on the reins. When we caught up with them, he'd slow down as soon as he got in front. Often, our bunch would canter along the road at a good pace, but when the rest turned off to another road, he would slacken his speed and mosey along. I'd have to prod him the rest of the way home."

Billy and I were approximately nine and ten years old, too small to perform the grooming and other tasks involved in caring for Fred. Glenwood or Lucille would lift us up high so we could scratch behind his ears and rub his face. When we stood on the ground and fed him some corn or an apple, we could feel his velvety nose and lips. We loved him!

Uncle Herman also had a gentle mule, Kate. She was a "ridin' mule." In addition to her work pulling the wagon and the plow, she would be saddled and ridden whenever Fred was not available, or if two people had to ride somewhere, one rode Fred the other rode Kate. She was about Fred's height, more compact and more muscular. Her coloring was mostly brown changing to gray at her chest and abdomen. She didn't have a blaze down her nose but her hair was lighter there. Her close clipped mane was black, so was her tail and the lower part of her legs near her hoofs. She was small but good at work with a single plow or wagon. During the seasons when everyone and everything on the farm was pressed into service for planting, hauling, or harvesting, she was just the right size to make a team with Fred. We liked her!

Kate was quite docile. She endured and may have enjoyed any attention Aunt Linnie's boys gave her. She, like Fred, seemed to like being groomed, but you stayed a respectful distance to the side and watched for signs of restlessness while doing so. She was not known to bite, but apples were put on the ground near her so she could get them herself. Corn was given to her from the end of a long ear. Occasionally we were lifted up to scratch the rough hair behind her ears, but we were warned not to touch the ears themselves. "Kate is mighty touchy about her ears!"

She was skittish when anyone got behind her. We were warned, "You better be careful not to get too close to Kate's heels. She's mighty touchy about them too!"

We learned that she was mighty touchy about something else as well, her meals. The working animals got feed, fresh water and rest, when the family and "hands" came from the fields at noon for dinner. Kate had learned the sound and purpose of the dinner bell. It was well known that wherever she was, plowing, pulling a wagon, or being ridden on some errand, she would quit what she was doing and head for the stable.

Once, when Uncle Eddy was plowing, he didn't hear the bell. Kate just turned around and started home. The plow fell over on its side and Uncle Eddy was jerked off his feet. The reins were wound around his hand and wrist so he couldn't let go. He wasn't able to release his hands until he had been pulled out of the field, over a bank, and almost into the creek. He walked to the house, dirty and bedraggled, but not hurt. Kate dragged the plow through the creek and all the way to the stable and her feed trough. There was hilarious laughter about it all through the dinner hour. Each witness to the event had a different tale to tell.

Most of the time during our visits Jim went off somewhere, Elbert and Earl went to school, and Billy and I stayed around the house during the day.

Aunt Linnie, Lucille, Uncle Eddy's daughter Mamie, and Mom were usually cooking, canning, or sewing. Billy and I amused ourselves chasing the cats and kittens around the henhouse or smokehouse. We explored the hayloft in the stable when someone was on the front porch to watch us or hear us if we called. Sometimes we played by the pond at the edge of the stable yard with a wary eye out for moccasins, either copperhead or cottonmouth. We skipped rocks across the water and watched frogs jump from the bank into the pond when we startled them.

Occasionally, when the grownups were too busy to keep their eyes on us, Lucille would get a bridle and take us to the pasture to get Fred. There was a tack house by the gate to the stable yard where the saddles and bridles were kept. She would lead Fred to the gate, saddle him, and put Billy and me up on his back.

Over the years we were coached, while sitting in front of Glenwood or Lucille on the saddle, with their hands over ours on the bridle. We learned to neck rein Fred to make him turn. We also learned to tug the reins sharply from one side or the other so the bit in his mouth would pull on his jaw and turn him that way. We learned to make a tch-tching sound from the side of our mouths to get him to start or go faster. If that didn't work we learned to kick him firmly on his sides to urge him on. I doubt that our firm kicking did much good since Fred was used to grown men and large boys, and Billy and I each weighed less than sixty pounds. The first thing we learned was to pull back hard on the reins to get him to stop.

We felt that we were experienced and able enough to ride by ourselves and were extremely confident when we were told to go on. Years later I realized that Mother and Aunt Linnie had very little confidence in us but they had an abiding faith in Fred.

First we went a mile or so up the dirt road to the one-room school where Elbert and Earl were. If it were lunchtime or they were having a play period, we would sit and watch while they played what they called "Town Ball." It was a cross between baseball and tag. A pitcher would pitch the softball to a batter. If he missed, it was a strike. If someone caught a fly ball, it was an out. If the batter hit a grounder, he ran around a base and back "home." Whoever picked up the ball would try to tag him with it before he reached "home." There was a lot of excitement during the game.

When the bell rang for classes to resume, Elbert would whack Fred on the rump and he would dart away. The first time Elbert did it, Billy and I almost fell off the horse, but we managed to stay on and got a good fast ride back to the house.

If the children were having classes, Billy and I would just turn at the schoolhouse and go back another mile or so the other way to a big tree stump where the road divided going around on each side of the stump. Fred learned the route so well he automatically went 'round the stump and headed back the other way. We seldom had to use the reins. Once in a while we met another horse and rider. Sometimes we had to make way for a wagon. I don't remember ever meeting any cars. Some of the farmers, including Uncle Herman, had them but they didn't use them often.

We loved to ride at a canter. The smooth rocking motion

was comfortable for us and, I think, easy on Fred. We were cautioned never to come back to the house or stable at a gallop. Uncle Herman said, "It's not good to let him get used to running home. Linnie and Lucille use him when they drive the buckboard or carriage. They aren't strong enough to control an excited horse."

Usually we rode double. Lucille made him stand close and parallel to the wooden gate while we climbed to the top rail and slid over onto his back.

We argued over which of us would sit in the saddle, hold the reins and "drive" Fred, and which of us would sit behind on Fred's bare back, holding on to the "driver."

Later, we began taking turns by "making" Fred stand close to the big stump at the divide in the road while we climbed off and on him again to change about.

One time, when Kate wasn't being used in the fields, Lucille saddled her as well as Fred, and we each had our own mount. Kate usually followed along with Fred about a head back. She turned when he turned, sped up when he sped, and stopped when he stopped. When Lucille had tightened the last cinch on Kate, Mother stated, "Now you two won't have to argue about who will 'drive' the horse!"

This was not really a solution to the problem.

Even though everyone knew that Kate was not easy to ride, I knew that protesting would do no good. It would probably end our chance to ride at all. Mother decided that Billy would ride on Fred. "He is younger." I got on Kate.

Fred was a saddle horse with several gaits. He cantered easily and rode fairly smoothly at a trot. Even with our short legs we could ride him comfortably.

Kate, though docile and willing, had only one gait, a stiff-legged trot. She trotted fast, she trotted slow, but she trotted. My legs were too short to reach the stirrups on any of the saddles. Even when Lucille shortened the leathers as far as possible, I could barely put my toes into the loop holding the stirrups. She said, "That's enough to keep you from falling off."

I jounced up and jolted down with every step Kate took. I couldn't stand up on the leathers to ease the bumps. I just had to sit there and be jounced and jolted. By the time we got to the schoolhouse I was in agony. My back was tired! My neck was tired! My bottom was tired and my head ached!

While we were circling around at the schoolhouse, I persuaded Bill to promise to change to Kate at the stump. We made what was for me a grueling ride to the changing point. I was sure that my tailbone, hipbone, and ribs were getting chipped at the edges from banging together each time I plunked down on the saddle. At last we halted at the stump.

I slipped off Kate, careful of my "chipped bones" and cautious of her big hoofs. I coaxed her over to the stump where Billy was waiting and held her head while he got on her. He said he would wait until I was on Fred before he started back.

I was standing on the stump leaning over Fred, reins in hand, putting my foot in the loop of the stirrup leather when the dinner bell rang! Kate took off. Fred saw her move and started after her.

I was caught with all my weight on the stirrup leather, and the saddle slipped. I threw myself down across Fred's back as the saddle turned down under him, stirrups dragging on the ground. Ordinarily Fred would have stopped, but his eyes were on Kate trotting in the lead! He must have been aware of the saddle suspended beneath his stomach because he merely began a fast trot after her. Any other gait would probably have tangled his feet in the stirrups.

I clung to the saddle girth with all my might, the long loose reins still clutched in my right hand. It took both hands over on his right side holding on to the leather girth to keep me from falling down into the path of Fred's hoofs, so I couldn't pull on the reins. I had landed on the bony vertebrae at his withers and was certain that my whole rib cage would crack asunder, but a few bounces brought me down to the curve of his back where I jiggled and jostled on my dinner. I was glad that I had eaten well because it provided a cushion between his backbone and my spine and, although I seemed to squish and squash, I didn't hurt. My feet and legs bobbled on his left side and my chest and abdomen bounced on his broad back.

Fred had caught up with Kate and they had assumed the appropriate sedate speed by the time we neared the gate where we could get off. Billy was all jostled out and glad for Uncle Herman to lift him down off Kate. A neighbor's urgent need had prompted the taps of the dinner bell that had called Uncle Herman from the field, and, inadvertently, Kate from our ride.

When I became aware that I was all right, I realized how funny the situation was and giggled as I jiggled the last hundred yards to the gate where Fred stopped and I slid to the ground laughing.

When she saw my undignified arrival, no visible torso — just my round rump in the middle of the horse's back, with legs all akimbo bobbing and kicking at his side — and the bulky saddle hanging underneath, Mother ran down from the house. She said she had been half-alarmed and three-quarters amused at the way I rode in, so when she saw me land on my feet she too burst into laughter.

Billy and I were not sorry that Kate was too busy with the plowing for us to ride her again that summer. Whenever Billy and I rode again, Lucille made sure that the saddle girth was good and tight. We also quit arguing and took turns at the reins more often. Fred is still one of our dearest and richest memories.

CHAPTER XVI

Ba-a-a Ba-a-a

Aunt Nancy took great pride in the little circular flower garden on the left side of the front yard. She also had a row of flowers along the fence on the left next to the orchard and the beehives. On the few occasions when Uncle Billy pastured the sheep in the field at the front of the house we children were told to be sure the front gate was closed after we entered or left the yard. Mom cautioned us, "The sheep are quick and could come in and destroy Aunt Nancy's flowers in a few minutes."

We were good about closing the gate. Mom had used her "or else" voice when she gave her instructions. However, one day when we were following Uncle Billy around at the stable we saw that he had brought two of his steers out of the pasture and put them into stalls in the stable. We asked him why he had them there. He said, "I'm goin' ta hitch 'em up an' do a job fer a fella up the road toward New

Bethel after dinner." Billy and I had seen horses and mules in various combinations hitched to wagons and other farm implements, but we had never seen steers harnessed to work. Excited, we raced back to the house to tell Mom, and in our excitement forgot the gate.

No one paid attention to us as we reached the porch yelling out our news. Mother dashed out of the parlor looking over our heads and shouting. Aunt Nancy swooped out of the front room with a broom, "Hey! Hey! Get out o' there." Billy and I looked around and there were the sheep, all of them. Myrtle Mae came from the back yard and plunged into the midst of a bunch headed her way and shooed them past the hollyhocks, sweet williams and coxcombs that lined the orchard fence. Mother's foray sent them off from the roses, daises, zinnias, and marigolds in the circular bed. Aunt Nancy and her broom rounded them up and out from the grape vines along the garden fence on the right. In a trice they were all herded back out into the pasture. Billy and I stood agape. We had almost forgotten what we were so anxious to tell.

Myrtle Mae and Aunt Nancy went back to the tasks they had left so precipitously. Mother faced us sternly. "What have I told you?" She didn't have to say more. Billy and I were as contrite as we could possibly be. We couldn't even express how sorry we were. It was a long time before we could approach her to tell her what had made us so excited.

Billy and I were unusually quiet at dinner until Aunt Nancy looked at us and said, "I just came in from the front yard. We got the sheep out before they did much damage to the flowers. A few of the daisies and zinnias were nipped off but the sheep didn't seem to like the marigolds. Myrtle got them away from the flowers on the side and the grapes were too high for them to reach."

With relief at that gesture of forgiveness, Billy and I got back to our usual chatter, including our excitement over the team of oxen.

Uncle Billy and all the adults rested after we had eaten. Billy and I dawdled around the woodpile, sat in the swing, picked up apples in the orchard, threw spoiled ones into the gully at the back, and busied ourselves near the house so we wouldn't miss Uncle Billy when he went to the barn.

At last he called us, "C'm on now. If yuh want ta watch."

We scampered off to the stable ahead of him and waited by the gates to the stalls the steers were in. Uncle Billy went into the tack room and brought out the queerest bunch of wooden things I had ever seen. In his hands he carried a long wooden bar, hand hewn and shaped into a low arc near each end, with holes drilled at either side of the arcs. A large heavy iron ring was bolted to the center of the square part of the bar.

Over his arm he carried two wooden things shaped like arches. Smooth, almost polished, they looked much like the hames that fitted over a horse collar. We watched as he coaxed the steers to stand side by side and eased the wooden bar onto their necks just in front of their shoulders.

"I bet Mark and Beck wouldn't stand that still while you put that thing on them," Billy stated.

"No. I reckon not," Uncle Billy replied. "Steers ain't neer' as skittish as horses and mules. They don't get upset easy. Besides, I been handlin' these steers since they was sucklin' calves. Rubbed 'em an' talked to 'em. I always carry grain in my pocket when I'm out in the field. Sometimes I'd coax 'em to me an' give 'em a little now an' then— one at a time o'course. Gradually I got 'em together an' got 'em used ta each other as well as me. They're real used ta me now. I've worked 'em together enough that they'll do or try most anythin' I tell 'em to."

He pushed one of the arches up under the neck of the steer on the left and worked the ends into the holes on each side of its neck. He did the same with the steer on the right. Tying a rope to the horn of one of the steers he gave it a slight tug, and sounding a "tks, tks, tks," with his tongue he said, "come along now." The steers moved out slowly behind him.

While they walked toward the tack room he explained, "The feller I'm goin' ta see got his wagon stuck in a mud hole and his team couldn't pull it out. He added another brace of mules but that didn't work either. He asked if I thought my steers could do it. We're goin' ta try."

Stopping at the door to the tack room, he commented, "These are young steers. I haven't worked 'em much. I don't know if they'll be strong enough to do the job."

He stepped up into the room. "It's a hot day. I'll need to put a collar and sweat pad on 'em."

The collar he took off a peg on the wall looked like the leather one he used for the mule. So did the heavy sweat pad he took down next.

Mother called us from the house. "We're going to visit Mr. and Mrs. Lewis, Nellie Cash's mother and father. Come in and get cleaned up." Reluctantly, we dragged off up to the house.

By the time we were dressed and started up the lane to the road, Uncle Billy had taken his team of oxen and gone. We never got to see him get all the harness on the steers.

The road to the Lewis' place went past the house where Russell Cash lived, but no one was out front to wave at. Billy and I kept our eyes on the dusty road and counted the wiggly snake tracks that wandered across it from one side to the other. I always wondered which way the snake went, from left to right or right to left. In any case, I watched the edges of the road carefully lest one had lingered at the side, but never saw any.

When we rounded the curve beyond Russell's house, we came upon a steep hill off to the left. A tall log house with a faded red tin roof was at the crest. I looked carefully at the house while we trudged up the deeply rutted roadway leading to it.

At home Billy and I created pioneer houses or western ranch cabins with our set of Lincoln Logs, and made up stories around the structures we had built. I had not imagined that people still lived in log dwellings. This one looked dark and gloomy, but it couldn't be that if the cheerful voices of Mr. and Mrs. Lewis who awaited us on the porch were any indication. Straight chairs with split cane seats had been set out for the adults. After we had been shown off, comments made about how much we had grown, and questions asked about where we were in school, the adults sat down to visit. We children sat on the porch floor with our feet dangling off the edge.

I spent my time looking closely at the house. Our Lincoln Logs were smooth and round with squared off

WHERE THE TWENTIES WEREN'T ROARING

notches at the ends that held the logs together by fitting at right angles. At the corners about a half-inch of the log extended beyond the union in each direction. No crack showed between one log and the next either. These logs were different. They were huge, square, and rough, with axe marks showing. Some kind of cement or plaster showed between each layer of logs. Instead of squared off notches these had a V-shaped groove that held an upside down A-shaped wedge. The corners met in smooth right angles. The V-shaped notches seemed to hold just as well as those of the Lincoln Logs, because this house was sturdy and looked like it had been standing there a hundred years.

After a time, Billy and I got thirsty so Mrs. Lewis took us through the house to the kitchen for a drink of water. As we went through the front room, I was surprised to see that the ceiling was about normal height. The red tin roof had been so tall and steep I thought the room would have a really high ceiling. Then I noticed a set of stairs in the corner. Like those at Uncle Billy's they started in the corner and went up three steps to a door. I knew that they began to turn at the door and go on to a room above.

A coal oil lamp sat on a pretty white lacy cloth atop a small table by the wall under the stairs. On the opposite wall was a small brick fireplace with andirons, and ashes in it. Mornings were still cool here. A ladder-backed rocker with a rush-bottomed seat was placed between the fireplace and the front window. A folded quilt rested on a large trunk under the window by the front door. In the corner by the back wall near the fireplace I saw the bed. It had a colorful quilt over it and a long pillow, the full width of the bed. I later learned that it was called a bolster and that Mrs. Lewis had tatted the lace on the cover.

The kitchen was like a shed attached to the back of the house. It was a double-boxed room and the ceiling was lower than that of the log room. A pie safe was at one end of the kitchen. At right angles to the safe was a cabinet with a board half pulled out from the work surface, much like the one Aunt Nancy had. Aunt Nancy's had a porcelain top where she rolled out biscuits in the mornings. There were two doors at the top and two drawers with curved bottoms below the work surface. Aunt Nancy kept flour and cornmeal in hers. The little iron cookstove at the back of the kitchen beside the door was like Aunt Nancy's. It stood on legs on a metal floor cover. There were four lids and a water reservoir at the back. A stovepipe ran straight up to the roof and out a chimney.

Mrs. Lewis took the wooden water bucket from a stand beside the door and went outside and emptied it into one of the old pots she used for watering the chickens. She set it down beside the cistern and lifted the metal bucket sitting on the wooden top, took off the top, and threw the bucket down into it. There was a big splash when the bucket hit the water. We all peered over the edge of the cistern to see if the bucket had turned over to fill with water. (Sometimes buckets just floated and had to be pulled up and thrown again.) The bucket filled and with another splash began to rise as she pulled the rope hand over hand until she could grasp the bale of the bucket. She poured the water into the wooden bucket and handed Billy the dipper to get his drink. He must have been truly parched. I thought I'd never get my turn. Before I finally got my chance, we went back into the kitchen, where she placed the wooden bucket back on the little table. At last I savored the clear cool taste of the water and noticed the little metallic tang from the dipper as I drank. By the time we got back to the porch Mother was standing up saying her good byes.

When we came back down the lane after our visit, we saw Uncle Billy coming up from the stable. With a triumphant grin he said, "Well, they did it. I was real proud of 'em."

He went over and met William and Jim coming from the woods back of the orchard. Jim had been following William at work most of the day. As they came up to where the sheep were grazing, William and Uncle Billy paused and studied the sheep. They exchanged a few words. Then William went over and picked up one of the lambs and carried it into the yard and out behind the house. I wondered what he would do with it.

Mother went inside and said a few words to Aunt Nancy. Then she came out to Billy and me and said, "We'll take a little walk down the hill to the melon patch. It may be too early for them to be ripe, but we can go see."

As we went out of the gate, I heard the lamb bleat once. Then there was no sound.

The melon patch was near the house, and we found no ripe ones. It seemed like no time until we came back to the house.

Mother said, "I think we can go back and see what William has done with the lamb." There it was hanging on a limb in the apple tree near the back steps behind the house. The hind legs were tied about a foot and a half apart. Its head was dangling near the ground. Its throat was cut clear across, and a bucket was under the head. William had already taken a sharp knife and cut the hide from the hoof of each leg to the center of the body and down the center of the body to the lower hooves. He was busy pulling the hide away from the legs and cutting the thin white tissue that seemed to hold the hide to the muscle beneath. Billy and I watched a little and then went back around to the swing at the front of the house. Jim stayed a little longer but he soon came to the front too.

Later, mother explained that someone had paid to have

the lamb butchered and brought to him. The lamb from Uncle Billy and one of his own pigs would provide the meat for the barbecue he was having that weekend. She also explained that selling the animals was one of the ways farmers got the money to run the farm and buy things for the family.

I was glad that she had taken us away so we would not see William kill the little lamb. I was not too young to understand that sometimes farmers had to do things they'd really rather not do.

CHAPTER XVII

Meetin', Eatin', an' Preachin'

Camp Meeting was a big religious revival and a grand homecoming for the folks of Lyon County, its surrounding counties, and all the former residents who had moved from the area to any other of the forty-eight states that existed at that time. It was held at the Kuttawa Mineral Springs during the second and third weeks of August. Dad always tried to get his vacation then so that he and Mother could attend.

Noted evangelists, ministers, and singers conducted the services. Preaching was at ten in the morning, one-thirty or two in the afternoon, and then about seven or seven-thirty at night on Sundays. During the week, services were held only in the evening.

Townspeople, guests of the Kuttawa Mineral Springs Hotel on the crest of the hill, and those who had rented the little yellow cabins on the hillside above the Pavilion where the "preachin'" took place, attended the evening services.

Farmer folk like our relatives went to the morning and afternoon services on Sunday. Their teen-agers and young adults would come back to evening services if they could arrange transportation. Since a lot of serious "courtin'" took place during camp meeting, parents would usually let the older boys take the buggy, or wagon or car if they had one.

We were usually at Uncle Billy's on the Sundays we went to the meeting. The days turned out to be long and arduous, but worth every bit of the effort for both young and old.

The grownups would have gotten up "before light" to begin preparations. Cows had to be milked. Chickens were fed and let out of the henhouse to forage around the flowerbeds and in the garden. Livestock were given their daily portion of grain and put out to pasture. Mark, Uncle Billy's bay horse, and Beck, his brown mule, were curried down and their hooves checked. The wagon was swept out so that no dirt or scraps of hay would soil the ladies' dresses or, for that matter, soil the men's clothes either. The team was hitched to the wagon and left tied in a shady place near the stable.

Chickens, which had been penned in coops and specially fed for several days, were killed, plucked, cut up, washed in salt water, floured, and plopped into skillets of hot bacon grease or lard to fry. Potatoes were boiled and peppers, green onions, pimentos, and celery were cut for potato salad. Mother deviled some eggs while Grandmother baked biscuits and Myrtle Mae baked a cake. An apple pie, baked yesterday, was already waiting in the pie safe.

By sun up all was well under way. Final touches were made to the food; the chicken was put on a couple of plates and wrapped tightly with a linen towel; the rest of the food was stored in baskets and boxes. A box containing a couple of old quilts and a few tablecloths was placed with the picnic things.

Now the cleanup began. Everybody retreated to the various sleeping rooms with wash pans of warm water, cloths, and towels. In a little while they emerged. The men were first, with crispy clean overalls, trousers or jeans, white shirts, ties, and carefully combed hair. Uncle Billy went down to the barn and drove the wagon to the house.

Pretty soon the women came out. They, too, were dressed in their best clothes. Aunt Nancy and Myrtle Mae had bought the material from Sears and Roebuck and made theirs. Mother had brought her good dress from home. Myrtle Mae and I came down last. I had given myself several licks and promises with the wash cloth and put on my clothes, while Myrtle Mae made careful preparations and checked her new dress to be sure it hung just right. My shiny face looked good to me but Myrtle Mae took a lot of time putting on powder, rouge, lipstick, and toilet water. Mother took me aside to re-clean some of my "promises" and comb my hair again.

Aunt Nancy was going back and forth from the kitchen to the porch overseeing the removal of the picnic boxes. She was tall, about as tall as Dad, who, Mother said, was between five feet ten and five feet eleven inches. Highly skilled at sewing, she had selected a pattern for her new dress that suited her large frame and covered it gracefully. The collar and bodice fitted well yet allowed enough fullness in the shoulders to permit her to use her arms freely. Although the style of the time was to have short skirts, hers came down almost to her ankles. That's what she was used to.

When Myrtle Mae entered the room wearing the dress she had made, Aunt Nancy looked at her critically. Eyes alight with approval and smiling her tight-lipped smile, she said, "It turned out well. It looks good on you. I think you were right to use the A-line skirt from that other pattern after all."

Aunt Nancy was creative herself and encouraged all her children, especially Myrtle Mae, to try out their own ideas. Sometimes things didn't turn out quite right. They were both pleased this time.

When we all got outside, Uncle Billy went 'round and climbed up to the wagon seat. Aunt Nancy broke into a wide smile as Dad offered to help her into the wagon to take her place beside Uncle Billy. He helped Grandmother, too.

A board had been fastened across the sides of the wagon just behind the regular seat. Dad also helped Myrtle Mae and Mother and then sat with them. William, Jim, Billy, and I sat on quilts placed on the floor of the wagon bed. By now it was after seven o'clock. Uncle Billy reckoned it would take us about an hour and a half to get to the springs. That would give us time to find a place to park the wagon and get in a little visiting before the morning service.

Everyone was looking forward to the events of the day. Aunt Nancy was a staunch Baptist and was looking forward to the sermon. The preacher this year was a noted Baptist evangelist. Mother once said that when Aunt Nancy was young she seldom missed any revival in the area. However, once she was "saved" she became more selective. Camp meeting was one revival she always attended. I am sure that Dad and Mother were as interested in the people they would see as they were in the revival itself. I suppose that the rest of us, if they were like me, were just looking for a good time.

Aunt Nancy remarked that Mark and Beck were not a well-matched pair, but Uncle Billy replied that there were few teams that worked together as well as they did. The sun was well up in the sky and we were already hot. Springs on the wagon seat eased the ride for Uncle Billy, Grandmother, and Aunt Nancy. Those of us on the wagon bed and the plank seat were jarred and shaken by every bump in the road. Dust swirled from beneath the hoofs of the team and the wheels of the wagon. Aunt Nancy had brought her big black parasol, which she raised to shade herself and Grandmother. Myrtle Mae on the plank seat behind them had raised her smaller sun-faded red one. The ladies each fanned themselves with palm frond fans that Aunt Nancy had also brought from home. There would be fans with light wooden handles advertising the Glenn Funeral Home under the pavilion at the camp grounds, but these fans were larger and stirred more air. The men wiped their faces with handkerchiefs. Jim, Bill, and I just endured.

A couple of buggies, a buckboard or two, and one surrey passed us as we rode along. Even though they drove past slowly, the amount of dust was doubled and rose in the gentle morning breeze to make us cough and sneeze and turn our heads.

There were a few low hills on the way, but other than tilting us a little more this way and that they didn't make us uncomfortable until we reached the long steep hill just before we got to the springs. I looked down the steep incline and wondered how we could keep from falling out.

Those on the seats had to lean way back and brace themselves. Jim, Billy, and I turned to face forward and held on to the sides of the wagon box. Uncle Billy pulled the lever that held the brake shoe against the wheel with all his might to keep the wagon from running up on the team. Mark's ears perked forward. Beck's long ears pointed back. Both heads rose more erect as their haunches lowered and their hooves dug into the dirt and gravel trying to slow the progress of the wagon. Somehow the harness was attached to the hames resting on the collar at their neck and chest and also to the wagon tongue, the trace chains, and the singletrees in such a way that the team could restrain the forward movement of the wagon. They breathed heavily and tossed and shook their heads as they struggled down the hill. I thought they were probably glad that we were not a load of tobacco. In fact, I wondered if this hill weren't the reason that Uncle Billy usually took his tobacco to the markets at Fredonia or Hopkinsville rather than Kuttawa.

The turn off to the campgrounds was at the bottom of the hill just after our road joined the Dycusburg road leading to the northwest. Aunt Nancy pointed out a nice spot not too far from the springs where the ground was flat, the grass was lush, and there was a little shade. The area nearer the springs was usually damp and soggy and would be unfit for spreading the picnic things on the ground at lunchtime.

Another wagon pulled in beside us and everyone exclaimed with joy. It was Myrtle Mae's sister, Isabel, with her husband, Jeff, and their little boy. They settled just far enough away to prohibit anyone's parking between the wagons. That way there would be a good picnic spot a few feet in front of the teams. It was agreed that we would "take dinner together" at noon. As the morning wore on there were several other families that decided to "take dinner" with us.

As if it had been planned, our group scattered when we got out of the wagon. The men gravitated over toward the barbecue restaurant where there were a lot of other men. The women went to some benches at a shady spot near the springs.

A little creek, formed high on the hill, flowed about twenty yards beyond the site of the mineral springs. Jim, Billy, and William joined a group of young men at the bridge over the creek who were watching a stick float down the stream until it disappeared behind the restaurant. Myrtle

Mae, with me tagging along, joined the teenaged girls standing under a huge oak tree not far from the spring.

A concrete wall with an iron railing on the top to keep people from falling into the water enclosed the spring itself. Evidently some of the young people had made a wishing well of it. There were pennies, nickels, and dimes visible on the bottom. Either the economics of the time or the strength of the wishes were such that I saw no quarters or half dollars among the change.

The girls were discussing their new dresses. Some bought their material from Sears as Myrtle Mae had. Others had gotten theirs from Gresham's store in Eddyville, Howerton's in Fredonia, or if they were lucky, from Princeton. Patterns may have come from the stores where they bought their cloth or from one of the magazines their mothers had. The *Delineator* and *The Modern Priscella* contained pictures advertising patterns that could be ordered from the magazine.

Some had made their dresses exactly by the pattern. Some, like Myrtle Mae, had combined patterns. My cousin Lucille didn't like the collar on the pattern she had, so she took a sheet of newspaper, laid it over the collar she liked on one of her winter dresses, cut her own pattern and used it. "I had to baste it in three times before I got it right, but it worked," she said.

About the time the discussion of the dresses came to an end, the bell at the Pavilion began to ring. From all sides of the hill the people turned to go to the morning worship. The family men caught up with their wives and children, courting couples went together, the cluster of young unattached ladies and teenaged girls followed them. The young men and boys sauntered up to take their stand on the periphery of the gathering. A few went on stage to sing in the choir.

By the time we had begun to cross the bridge, I could

hear singing from the Pavilion. "We're marching to Zion. Beautiful, beautiful Zion." I was surprised to hear the sound of guitars, fiddles, a banjo, and a mandolin playing the hymns along with the piano.

The Pavilion was a huge open-sided structure with a tin roof supported by pillars made of tree trunks about eight inches thick with the bark peeled off. The whole Pavilion was gleaming with fresh whitewash.

The crowd was singing "I'm on the Sunny Side" when we went up the steps on the right side of the stage to be in the choir. I looked out into the Pavilion and saw row after row of people sitting on long benches on each side of a middle aisle. The whole front row was empty. The stage went all across the front. In the center, which was backed by a wooden wall, there were several men seated near a podium. One man held a large Bible on his knee. The men with the instruments were on the left side of the stage.

A tall robust man with a loud voice was standing by the podium leading the singing. His voice carried to the back of the Pavilion and to the hillside beyond. There were no amplifiers then so it took a big voice to carry all that distance. On the floor level near the first row of benches in front of the stage, a skinny little man was playing the piano, his eyes glued to the singer.

The song leader called out the page number of "There Shall Be Showers of Blessings." With a flurry of runs and tremolos, the pianist played the last line of the refrain as an introduction. The man waved his hand and everyone began to play and sing. I'm sure that some of the farmers, concerned about the corn parching in the midsummer draught and mindful of the heavy dews that had sustained the crop thus far, sang the words "mercy drops 'round us are falling but for the showers we plead," with particular fervor and a more literal intent than the hymn writer had in mind.

A number of worn paperbacked song books with shaped notes were scattered among the "Choir" on the stage and among those sitting in the Pavilion. If they knew the words, those scattered on the hillside sang too. Almost everyone joined in at the refrains or choruses, which were repeated after each verse of most of the songs. I was able to keep up with the singing. Although I didn't know the songs and did not understand the shaped notes, I could read the words and catch the tune from Myrtle Mae. We closed the singing with "He Keeps Me Singing." Our leader told us how he loved the music and how the happy voices that joined him in singing had lifted his spirit. Then he sat down.

One by one the men on the platform, who were the local ministers showing their support of the Camp Meeting, rose and went to the podium to express their hope that this meeting would bring joy, a renewal of faith, and new followers of the Word of Christ. The last one introduced the preacher who would lead the revival.

The guest preacher acknowledged his introduction, mentioned his high regard of "Brothers so and so" who represented the various denominations that were gathered there and then he emphasized the brotherhood of all Christians. He greeted those in attendance and hoped he would stir their hearts during the two weeks and three Sundays of Revival services. Then he bent his head in a long prayer for the success of his mission.

At this time he asked the song leader to lead the people in some more songs in praise of the Lord.

The song leader asked the people to stand and called out the page number of "Dwelling in Beulah Land" and after that, "Standing on the Promises." I felt a tingling excitement each time a few resonant bass voices, bullfrog deep, chanted, "Standing on the promises. Standing on the promises" while we treble voices sang "Sta - - nd - ding, sta - - nd - ding," during the choruses. That hymn is still one of my favorites. Again the leader thanked everyone for the enthusiastic singing and went back to his seat.

Briskly striding forward, the local minister gestured for the audience to sit down. He praised the song leader and the piano player. Then he spoke of his anticipation of the message to come. "But before our Revivalist begins his sermon, we would like to take up a collection to help support this great meeting."

He called on several members of the assembly to come and get the small shallow baskets that they would use for the collection. After a short prayer some of the men began to move down the center and side aisles to pass the baskets among those under the Pavilion. Some went among those standing and sitting outside on the hill.

While the collection was being taken, the song leader turned to the choir and called for "Wonderful Words of Life." Again the pianist played a florid introduction and the choir and orchestra joined all together. The pianist's jazzy style with all the fancy variations, ornamentations, and modulations that he drew from the keyboard, added excitement to the hymn. To me, his playing compared favorably with the vaudeville musicians our family heard playing in the theatres back in Hammond. Many of the best vaudeville acts were booked there between their engagements in Chicago. When we reached the end of the last refrain, the song leader called out, "I'll Go Where You Want Me To Go." Without a pause and without changing the music, the pianist played a few ornamental runs and then struck out the last line of that song. The choir and instrumentalists made the shift of meter and key to continue singing and playing until the men with the baskets had made the complete round of those present. I wondered if the pianist knew the whole hymnbook by memory.

The collection having been received and blessed, the guest preacher rose, placed his Bible on the podium, and introduced the scripture he had chosen for the morning session. Pausing for a minute, he re-emphasized a few key words from the passage that he had chosen for his text. In a conversational tone he began to explain the historical setting and the episode from which the words of the text arose. In more earnest terms he set out to explain the meaning of the words in that context. With great enthusiasm he related the meaning of these ancient words to modern life and brought out the virtues that were explicit in Christian living. He ended his sermon with joyful exaltation. Then he invited those who did not know Christ to come forward and be saved by His grace. "Come, let me help you meet Jesus."

The song leader and the choir began quietly singing "Softly and Tenderly Jesus Is Calling" while the preacher descended the stairs on the right side of the stage and stood in the center of the aisle by the empty benches and repeated his invitation again and again.

After a while, since no one came to the front, the minister who had made the introduction, stood to praise the message and the messenger. He reminded the people of the afternoon preaching at two o'clock and gave the benediction.

The morning session over, we all headed back to the wagon for dinner.

Our whole party gathered quickly at the wagon. Some of the men took empty jugs to the springs to bring back the cool mineral water to drink. Several tin or enamel cups were placed near them. Mother took the collapsible cup from her purse for our family to use. Myrtle Mae and I spread a quilt over the grass to smooth it out. On top of that we spread a white tablecloth. Mother, Grandmother, and Myrtle Mae got the pie, the cake, the chicken, the potato salad, the bean salad, sliced tomatoes, sliced cucumbers, and biscuits from the various boxes and placed them on the tablecloth. Aunt Nancy got out the plates and bone handled knives and forks to put at one end. Isabel brought the things she had prepared and set them out. Someone else laid a cloth next to Aunt Nancy's. Soon it was filled with food from that family.

Another group placed their things nearby and exchanged conversation and invitations to share. It was probably Aunt Linnie and Uncle Herman, or Nellie and Leonard Cash, or Teely and Lysander Lamb and their families. They were all neighbors or relatives who enjoyed being together and sharing the work and the food.

In our group, after Uncle Billy said a short blessing, the men were told to help themselves. It didn't matter whose food they took. Everyone shared gladly. When the men had filled their plates and gone to a shady spot to eat, the women and children took their turn. Mother helped Billy and me, since we couldn't handle our plates and reach for food too. She also knew the things I would eat. I was a finicky eater and she didn't want any food to be wasted.

I had never seen such a bountiful spread in all my life. In addition to the staple foods each family had brought, there were layer cakes—coconut, chocolate with seven minute frosting, chocolate with chocolate icing, devil's food with chocolate icing, angel food with almond icing, sunshine with white icing, white with caramel icing, and others I can't recall.

There were pies—apple, peach, blackberry, lemon chess, chocolate chess, brown sugar, coconut cream, lemon meringue, and CHOCOLATE MERINGUE. There were several chocolate pies but I thought Isabel made the best. I made sure I got some of hers. To this day my mouth waters when I remember Isabel's chocolate pie.

When our plates were filled, we sat on the ground in little groups. The grown women sat a little apart from the men. I sat among the other little girls about my age, but I watched and tried to listen to the conversation of Myrtle Mae and her friends who were sitting to one side. Oddly, I don't remember the girls of my age. I was too interested in watching and listening to the older ones.

The men and the big and little boys separated the same way. Although we were seated in little groups, we were all close enough to exchange conversation and plenty of banter.

No one counted how many times anyone went back to the table. In fact the women were glad to see the food being enjoyed. One could go back to the table time and again, even for dessert, without being stopped. I probably quit with the piece of chocolate pie, not that I didn't want more, I simply couldn't hold more.

When the appetites seemed satisfied, some of the men drifted away to other parts of the campground. The rest of us helped with the cleaning. Plates were gathered up. If some food was left on a plate, it was scraped into a bucket or lard can to be taken home and fed to the pigs and chickens. If there were leftovers in a bowl, they were offered around. "Here, won't someone eat the rest of this potato salad? There are only about two bites left. It won't keep." Someone would volunteer. "Here's a chicken thigh that's left. Mr. Jimmy, you'd like that." Dad would accept the piece and comment on how long it had been since he had eaten enough fried chicken. There would be bits of this and that to be eaten by someone until the bowls and plates were emptied and put back into their baskets and boxes to be taken home. The tablecloths would be put away and the quilts placed back into the wagon. If they were damp from the ground or from something being spilled on them, they would be dry by the time we got home.

The meal having been disposed of, it was time to go about the hillside to visit with distant kin and friends that could be found there. Seeing someone they knew, Dad and Mother called us children to them and struck out for a group on the hill on the other side of the spring. On the way, they were met by others they were also glad to see. "I had hoped we would find you this year. Somehow we missed you last time." The man of the family, big, with iron gray hair and a graying beard asked, "Miss Georgie, do you remember the time you whupped me?"

Mother laughed and said, "Indeed I do. You boys just couldn't stay out of mischief. Where are your children now?" They would catch up on families. We three would be introduced and everyone would move on.

Mother and Dad both taught school in the area before they moved to Indiana. They must have been well liked, as former students would seek both of them for a few moments of greeting and reminiscence. So many of the men recalled the time that mother "whupped" them that Jim once remarked that "Mother must have whipped every old man in Kentucky." We finally reached the family on the hill. Mrs. Cordy Jones was unable to walk the uneven grounds, so her family stayed in that one place and their friends came to them. They were all close friends whom Mother and Dad used to visit when they were courting. There were many things to recall and much news to exchange.

Bill and I had become hot and thirsty so we asked if we could have a nickel for a bottle of pop. Dad said we could have one nickel but we would have to share the pop. All the way to the barbecue restaurant we argued. I wanted cherry and he wanted grape, or some different flavor, not cherry. Finally I decided that we should have something that neither of us had tried before. Coca-Cola was one drink our parents would not let us have. We were going by ourselves, so, being a true daughter of Eve, I suggested that we spend our nickel on a bottle of Coke! On that we both agreed.

All the fruit flavored sodas we had ever tried had a pleasant, sweet bubbly taste. I felt sure that Coca-Cola would be the most delicious drink in the world. The restaurant was dark, crowded, hot and noisy, so we took our bottle outside to drink. I got the first swallow. Wow! It wasn't sweet at all! It tasted like medicine and my tongue stung as if it had been stuck with needles. I swallowed my mouthful with difficulty and handed the bottle to Billy. He took one sip and spit it out on the grass at the side of the restaurant. Going out to the back, we poured the rest of it out onto the ground. Then we put the bottle in the crate beside the door and headed over to the spring. Cupping our hands, we dipped up a few sips of the cool water to wash out the foul taste in our mouths and went back up the hill to re-join our parents. We said no more about being thirsty that day. We had wasted our nickel.

In a little while the bell at the Pavilion began to ring and we went on to the afternoon service. I found my place on the stage in the choir between Myrtle May and my other cousin, Lucille, and joined them and the orchestra in the singing. We sang "What a Friend We Have in Jesus" and then, "In the Land Where You Never Grow Old." The singers probably had different mental pictures during that song—we youngsters thinking of perpetual youth and the older folk envisioning renewed mobility and freedom from worry and care. No matter, we all sang the refrain, "... Never grow old. Never grow old. In the land where we'll never grow old," with enthusiasm enough to make the hills around us echo.

There was not as much ceremony at the first of the

service as there had been that morning. The local minister welcomed us again and mentioned there were folks there who had missed the morning session. He praised the revival preacher and gave a prayer remembering all those that were present and their loved ones who had not been able to come, prayed for the messenger and hoped that he would stir our hearts with God's Word as he had done that morning. With that he invited the guest preacher to come to the podium.

This time he greeted those who had been there that morning and those who had come this afternoon and went straight to his text. He read passages that dealt with some of the miracles of Jesus. As he had done that morning, he explained them in the context of the Bible, and then showed their significance in modern lives and more specifically, the lives of those assembled there.

He called for another session of hymns while the offering was taken. We sang "Tell Me the Old, Old Story," "Trust and Obey," and "Let the Lower Lights Be Burning." Late-comers arrived and were seated as the offering baskets were passed.

The Pavilion had been comfortable in the morning, but it was hot and stuffy in the afternoon. Mother and Dad, Grandma and Uncle Billy sat on a quilt under the trees on the hillside. Aunt Nancy, her sister Tela, and Isabel sat in the Pavilion, their fans fluttering.

Though the sides were open to the air and the roof shaded us, it was hot in the choir. We were seated close together and the heat from our bodies augmented that from the sun. Even the breeze felt steamy. I missed much of the sermon. It was long and I got sleepy. I drowsed through a lot of it, leaning first on Myrtle Mae and then on Lucille.

I did hear enough to realize that the preacher was expounding on the lessons Jesus taught and the promises he made to us for the life hereafter. The sermon was more earnest than the jubilant message he gave that morning. This time instead of letting us merely rejoice that we were blessed as Christians, he pointed out our Christian duties and obligations.

Again those who did not know Christ were asked to come and accept him as their Savior. The musicians softly began the song, "Jesus, Keep Me Near the Cross," while the preacher descended to the floor and repeatedly invited those who were unhappy and living in sin to come to him.

No one responded to the invitation this time either, so the host minister rose and thanked the preacher, announcing that we should all return for the evening service at seven o'clock. He stated that he had been told that the subject would be the devil, Satan, and that we should not miss it! He then pronounced the benediction.

Slowly the crowd rose and noisily began to disperse. Some made their way to the hotel at the top of the hill or to the cabins. The rest made their way down past the spring to where the wagons, buggies, horses, or cars had been left. No one hurried. There were still people to greet. Mother and Dad stopped and chatted often. Uncle Billy, Grandma, and the rest of the family were already in the wagon when we got there. The summer days of August had begun to shorten and there were the chores and cleaning to do when we got back to the farm.

The little congestion at the intersection of the road to Kuttawa and Eddyville and the Dycusburg road soon thinned out and we began the hard climb up the steep hill at the edge of town. Although Mark and Beck had to strain at the harness, the trip up the hill was not as exciting as the trip down had been. The day was still hot and the road dusty. Even though we sometimes didn't see the wagons and buggies going ahead of us, the powdery clouds they had left behind had not yet settled when we came along.

We arrived home happy but hot, tired, grimy with dust, and there was still much to do. The wagon had to be unloaded, a fire started in the cookstove to heat water to wash the dishes, and the milking to be done. Fortunately, the cows had been left in the small field on the other side of the woods behind the barn. Myrtle Mae called them as she went down the path and they had come to the gate by the time she got there.

Uncle Billy and William went out to unhitch the wagon and the horse and mule. William fed Mark and got out the buckboard so he could harness him quickly when it was time to go back to the evening service.

Dad and Jim stayed at the house to carry the boxes in from the front gate where they had been set down from the wagon. Aunt Nancy, Grandmother, and Mom began unloading them and putting things away. When the water got hot, they gave me a washpan of cold water out of the cistern, put a little hot water in it and told me to clean myself for bedtime while they did the dishes. Mom took care of Bill.

By the time I had my pajamas on, everyone had gathered in the kitchen. It was almost beyond dusk, so the lamps had been lit. Amid the dark, moving shadows we cast on the walls we made our supper of the leftovers from the picnic and recounted scraps of conversation and bits of the sermons that were heard that day.

Myrtle Mae and William took Mark and the buggy and went back to the camp meeting. By then it was pitch dark and the rest of us were going to "turn in for the night." The steps leading to Myrtle Mae's bedroom upstairs were steep and the risers were high for my short legs, so Mother, picking up a lamp, helped me go up and tucked me into bed.

It had been a long day, from before sunup until after sundown. I was so tired I fell right to sleep and never even knew when William and Myrtle Mae came back from the meeting.

I never learned what the preacher said about Satan either. The next morning William and Myrtle Mae were too full of who was there and who went with whom. I think William did mention that someone must have acquainted the preacher with some local rumors. "He didn't name any names but he gave a good description of the lane leading to that woods over near Confederate, where there's supposed to be a still."

Memories aroused during the visits with the people around the spring, bits and pieces of conversations, the music and the sermons gave them all a lot to talk about until the next Sunday.

Dad was due back at work in a few days so we had to concentrate on packing our things for the trip home. It was like getting ready to come in reverse—the same hasty preparations, but without the joy and excited anticipation. The car was packed, we said our good-byes, climbed aboard, and retraced our route to Hammond. Billy and I never told that we had tasted a Coca-Cola.

CATHERINE DYCUS was born and raised in Hammond, Indiana, an industrial suburb of Chicago. She earned a B.A. degree at Iowa State Teacher's College (now the University of Northern Iowa) at Cedar Falls, Iowa, in 1942, and a M.A. degree at George Peabody College for Teachers (now part of Vanderbilt University) in Nashville, Tennessee, in 1955.

She has taught high school and elementary vocal and instrumental music, history and English. She retired as Supervisor of Music for the Newport News Public Schools in Newport News, Virginia, in 1979. She is active in the Lifelong Learning Society at Christopher Newport University in Newport News Virginia, sings in her church choir, travels, reads, and cares for her aging dog Tess.

To order additional copies, please use the coupon below.

Mail or fax to:

Brunswick Publishing Corporation
1386 LAWRENCEVILLE PLANK ROAD
LAWRENCEVILLE, VIRGINIA 23868
Tel: 434-848-3865 • Fax: 434-848-0607
www.brunswickbooks.com

Order Form
___ copy(s) of *Where the Twenties Weren't Roaring*
    by Catherine Dycus
    $16.95 ea., paperback .... $ _____
    VA residents add 4.5% sales tax
    ($.76 per copy) .... $ _____
    Shipping – within U.S. and Canada
    $5.00 1st copy .... $ _____
    $.50 ea. additional copy .... $ _____

    Total .... $ _____

❑ Check   ❑ Money Order enclosed.
❑ Charge to my credit card:
    ❑ VISA   ❑ MasterCard   ❑ American Express

Card #_____ Exp. Date _____
Signature: _____
Name_____
Address _____
City_____ State____ Zip _____
Phone # _____